THE NEW POPULISM

Democracy Stares into the Abyss

MARCO REVELLI

Translated by David Broder

VERSO

London • New York

This English-language edition published by Verso 2019
Originally published in Italian as *Populismo 2.0*
© Einaudi 2017
Translation © David Broder 2019

1 3 5 7 9 10 8 6 4 2

Verso
UK: 6 Meard Street, London W1F 0EG
US: 20 Jay Street, Suite 1010, Brooklyn, NY 11201
versobooks.com

Verso is the imprint of New Left Books

ISBN-13: 978-1-78873-450-9
ISBN-13: 978-1-78873-451-6 (UK EBK)
ISBN-13: 978-1-78873-452-3 (US EBK)

British Library Cataloguing in Publication Data
A catalogue record for this book is available from the British Library

Library of Congress Cataloging-in-Publication Data
A catalog record for this book is available from the Library of Congress

Typeset in Fournier MT by Hewer Text UK Ltd, Edinburgh
Printed and bound by CPI Group (UK) Ltd, CR0 4YY

Contents

1

Populism 2.0: Democracy's Senile Disorder

'A spectre is haunting the world: populism'. Thus claimed two leading humanities scholars, Ghita Ionescu and Ernest Gellner, in their introduction to what remains one of the most important and complete reviews of the populist phenomenon (*Populism: Its Meaning and National Character*).[1] Writing in the 1960s, they were here referring to the peripheral countries that were emerging from colonial domination and underdevelopment to chart their course toward independence.

A decade ago, this statement suddenly became relevant again – and this time it did not apply to the peripheral countries, but to the centre itself. Indeed, in 2012, the political scientist Ivan Krastev quoted it at the beginning of what has become something of a canonical work. In his essay, he illustrated his theses on what he called 'the populist moment', or rather, presented our time as 'the age of populism'. For Krastev, populism has become the most significant movement in contemporary politics.[2]

---

1 Ghita Ionescu and Ernest Gellner (eds.), *Populism. Its Meaning And National Characteristics*, London: Weidenfeld and Nicolson, 1969.

2 Ivan Krastev, 'The Populist Moment', *Critique & Humanism*, September 2007.

Today, however, this expression has taken on much more concrete meaning. The spectre has assumed bodily form – a massive, muscular figure – as so-called populism has dealt a series of heavy blows at the door of the Western democracies. They have followed one after another, from the Brexit referendum and Donald Trump's election in the United States in 2016 to the challenge mounted by Marine Le Pen and her Front National in the 2017 French presidential election, and the 'great fears' that this sparked. The latest blow came with the earthquake of the 4 March 2018 Italian elections and the establishment of an openly populist government in Rome. And that is not to mention the many smaller pieces of the puzzle, from Hungary to Poland, Slovakia, Slovenia and Austria: the countries along Europe's eastern spine where, falling like dominoes, one government after another has been conquered by political forces that can be classified – or in any case, have been classified – as 'populists'. And, here, this means a 'populism' riddled with xenophobia and strongly hostile to the last generation of civil rights measures.

Everywhere in the West, political systems have been shaken. They have been shaken by challengers that, while not taking an explicitly hostile stance toward democracy, seem to have risen from its bowels to point an accusing finger at some kind of deficit, and demand what Michel Foucault called its 'excedence'. In any case, these challengers are a dynamic force driving a rupture in all of democracy's established systemic balances. It is as if there were some unresolved, ambivalent link, combining complicity and conflict, between the institutional order of democracy and a challenge emanating from society itself. It is hard to predict the ultimate results of such a tension. Its outcome remains – often dramatically – uncertain, in a historical moment in which there is enormous pressure on politics itself (qua system for the authoritative regulation of social relations).

An odd couple . . .

The truth is that democracy and populism are interlinked by an unbreakable connection. An 'original' one: they have common roots. *Demos* in Greek and *populus* in Latin refer to the same subject: the people. And they thus refer to what is, in large part, a common destiny. For when the people 'are hurting', democracy suffers too . . .

Here, therefore, we will discuss populism first of all as a 'symptom' of a deeper illness – even if one we are too often silent about – of democracy itself. It is the outward manifestation of a sickness in the contemporary form of democracy – the only one that has established itself in modernity, erected over the ruins of participatory utopias – that is, representative democracy. Whenever some part of 'the people', or an entire people, *does not feel represented*, it returns to one or another kind of reaction that takes the name 'populism'. Early in democracy's development, this reaction appeared as its 'infantile disorder', when limited suffrage and class barriers kept part of the citizenry *out of* the game (late nineteenth- and early twentieth-century populism was, in large measure, a 'revolt of the excluded'). Today, it manifests itself as a 'senile disorder of democracy'. For the thinning-out of democratic processes and the return of oligarchic dynamics at the heart of the mature democracies marginalise or betray the mandate of a people whose 'sceptre'[3] of power has been taken

---

3 Daniel Albertazzi and Duncan McDonnell, 'The Sceptre and the Spectre', Introduction in *Twenty-First Century Populism: The Spectre of Western European Democracy*, New York: Palgrave MacMillan, 2008.

away. Post-twentieth-century populism is, in a sense, a 'revolt of the included' who have now been pushed to the margins. In both cases, what we might call the 'populist syndrome' is the product of a deficit of representation. For this reason, one recent scholar of populism used a particularly felicitous expression when he defined it as 'something like a permanent shadow of modern representative democracy'.[4]

A catch-all term . . .

It cannot be denied. The term 'populism', such as it is used in political debate and journalistic commentary today, has become almost unusable, given how imprecisely it is used and with such an enormous variety of meanings (all of them pejorative). As two authoritative scholars of this phenomenon have noted,[5] the definition of populism is a bit like the Welsh poet and playwright Dylan Thomas's sarcastic definition of an alcoholic as 'someone you don't like who drinks as much as you do': a populist is someone who uses a political style not much different from yours, but who you don't like . . .

We could also characterise 'populism' as a catch-all term that takes in all sorts of things as if they all shared some common essence. It takes in the old like the new, yesteryear's manifestations of radical protest like today's (or perhaps tomorrow's) forms of electoral revolt; the Russian populists of the nineteenth

---

4   Jan-Werner Müller, *What Is Populism?*, University of Pennsylvania Press, Philadelphia, 2016, p. 11.

5   Daniel Albertazzi and Duncan McDonnell, *The Sceptre and the Spectre*, Introduction in *Twenty-First Century Populism. The Spectre of Western European Democracy*, Palgrave MacMillan, New York, 2008.

century like the Italian *qualunquisti* of the late 1940s,[6] the British suffragettes of the turn of the twentieth century along with the sexist Trump voters in the age of American decline; the builders of walls under Viktor Orbán's command along with those searching out new paths for Europe, such as the Greeks behind Alexis Tsipras or the Spaniards behind Pablo Iglesias . . .[7] everything outside and (usually) *against* the so-called 'Establishment' (another catch-all term of loose definition). Too much – too many 'objects' – to stand under a single umbrella, however wide. Too many signifieds for one signifier. Or, rather, too many points of reference. As one scholar has written, 'Only a vague and ill-defined concept'[8] can take in such a wide repertoire of political phenomena; it thus risks doing nothing to help us understand them clearly.

So, first of all, we need to try to restore some order to our definitions themselves. And to set out some conceptual and chronological boundaries. At this point, we are talking about plural 'populisms' more than 'populism' in the singular, given the multiplicity of experiences that fall under this term, and which cannot

---

6 The *Fronte dell'Uomo qualunque* (Ordinary Man's Front) was a short-lived political party founded by Guglielmo Giannini (with an eponymous newspaper) that emerged in revolt against the anti-fascist parties that ruled Italy in the immediate aftermath of World War II.

7 On the uses and abuses of the term 'populism', as well as its use as a technical term within political science, note the far-reaching literature review based on the reflections of Isaiah Berlin, Richard Hofstadter and D. MacRae, 'To define populism' which appeared in 1968 in *Government and Opposition*, the authoritative journal founded three years previously. It also appeared in a volume the following year, edited by Ghita Ionescu and Ernest Gellner, *Populism*. See also the text by Margaret Canovan, *Populism*, Harcourt Brace Javonovich, New York, 1981.

8 Krastev, 'The Populist Moment'.

5

be reduced to a night in which all cows (or the farmers herding them) are black. We are distinguishing not only between the different 'populist experiences' but also between what we could call the classic, or traditional populisms – on which there now exists an extensive body of work, and some (if not a lot of) high-level historiographical reconstructions[9] – and the populism that is emerging today. Namely, what we here call 'populism 2.0', which is to say a new generation of populism, what we should call a second – or rather, 'third generation' populism in order to underline its new and unprecedented characteristics. Or the wholly new ways in which some of the traditional aspects of populism have been taken up again amidst the convulsions of the turn of the century. A new world that has been explored only in part.

Post-democracy . . .

But now we need directly to tackle the live matter of the malaise. We face a crisis of democracy (of representation, of legitimation, of sovereignty) without doubt much more serious than we are usually prepared to admit. The situation is serious enough that

---

9   On American populism, see Michael Kazin, *The Populist Persuasion: An American History*, Cornell University Press, Ithaca and London, 1998, perhaps the most complete reconstruction of the whole span of this history; see also the contributions by George McKenna, *American Populism*, Putnam, New York, 1974; Lawrence Goodwyn, *Democratic Promise*, Oxford University Press, Oxford, 1976; Robert McMath, *Populism. A Social History*, Hill & Wang, New York, 1992 and Charles Postel, *The Populist Vision*, Oxford University Press, Oxford, 2007; as well as Christopher Lasch's famous text, *The True and Only Heaven*, Norton, New York, 1991. For a European reading, see: Guy Hermet, *Les populismes dans le monde. Une histoire sociologique (XIXe–XXe siècles)*, Fayard, Paris, 2001.

for some time now we have been speaking in terms of 'post-democracy',[10] alluding to the somehow terminal character of today's illness: that is, to the ever more entrenched oligarchic distortion that democracy is subject to, whereby it becomes ever less representative and ever more 'executive'. We need to contend with the underlying social crisis, the real hypocentre – a point of deep rupture – of the earthquake that is shaking our political order; and so, too, challenge the way in which it has rapidly coalesced, redrawing the structure of classes and social groups with the widespread *déclassement* of the middle classes. We need to tackle the pulverisation of the so-called 'world of work', fragmented into a kaleidoscope of professional figures and identities that are no longer in dialogue with one another. And we must confront the impoverishment of what had been rising social strata of small privileged groups – both old and new – a phenomenon which presents worrying signs of a sudden change in the pace of the so-called 'social elevator' . . .

All this is happening in tandem with a sudden and troubling unravelling of the 'good manners', the relative tolerance and the 'civility' of political conflict, within which shell there played out a process of 'middle-classisation' (a horrible, but difficult-to-replace term)[11] of Western societies with their retinue of political

---

10   See Colin Crouch's pioneering study, *Coping with Post-Democracy*, published by the Fabian Society in 2000, subsequently followed by his *Post Democracy*, Polity Press, London, 2004.

11   The term was used by CENSIS in 2006 in its volume *Un'Italia articolata per ceti. Un mese di sociale 2006* (Franco Angeli, Milan, 2006) – see, on this Giuseppe De Rita's introduction – and then adopted in CENSIS, *La crisi della sovranità. Un mese di sociale 2012* (Franco Angeli, Milan, 2012). It has a particularly important explanatory role in the section dedicated to 'I rivolti sociali di una società fragile e eterodiretta' (p. 23), after which came

correctness, spirit of mediation and channelling of dissent through parliamentary channels. This had seemed to be a stable mechanism, but it is now being replaced by a rhetoric that seems 'politically incorrect' (and, as such, sincere, as opposed to the prevalent hypocrisy), aggressive (and thus direct), instantaneous and targeted (unlike the inconclusive discussions of what the reactionaries of the nineteenth century called the *clase discutidora*, in their term for the nascent liberal-parliamentary bourgeoisie).[12]

Ochlocracy, or, 'government by the plebs'

Looking at the thick new layer of social dust deposited at the foot of the social pyramid as the old 'blocs' or ('classes') that characterised the industrial epic have crumbled, we would be tempted to characterise it as belonging to the 'plebs'. 'Ochlocracy' – 'government by the plebs' – as Polybius called the degeneration of democracy when the value of equality is lost and the people seeks revenge[13] – is the kind of the government anticipated by this sort of 'social disaggregate', which bears the whole charge of rancour, frustration, intolerance and radicalism that *déclassement* and

---

the emptying out of 'the great lake of middleclassisation'. In De Rita's portrayal, 'middleclassisation' was not only a socio-economic process but also, and perhaps most importantly, an anthropological process produced by the 'rise of those who had been at the bottom of the social pyramid, as well as part of the old elite slipping down it'. 'Everyone is middle class', De Rita wrote, describing this condition before it entered into crisis. 'Remaining outside were a very small elite and the marginalised. What Pasolini would have called a bourgeoisified country, rendered fully conformist'.

12   An 1852 expression from Donoso Cortés, adopted by Carl Schmitt in his *Politische Theologie* (1922).

13   Polybius, *Histories*, fragment VI, 4.

disaggregation entail. It is as if a new socially barbarised population had suddenly emerged alongside – or better, from beneath – the good old people of yesterday's democratic rhetoric, supplanting and submerging it. These, then, would be the architects of Brexit – the rash types driving the Leave vote as against the prudent supporters of Remain, who the whole establishment around the world were cheering for; they are the protagonists of Trump's troubling victory, first in the primaries, which shattered the image and the leadership of the Grand Old Party, and then even – *horribile visu* – the presidential contest itself; they are the spectres haunting Europe, coming from the Left or (more often) from the Right to destabilise the oligarchic leadership of the European Commission and the European Union's institutions; they are the fuel driving *grillismo*, *lepenisme*, movements driving for independence from the euro, the revolt against TTIP as well as the revolt against immigrants. This is a sort of new Hyksos invasion – no longer on the national scale, like in Benedetto Croce's vision of the origins of Fascism in Italy, but now at a global or at least Western scale.

Or so things could be characterised, if such a formulaic representation of the phenomenon did not come up against the fact that this seemingly new protagonist also has a history. This formless multitude, whose repeated shifts today arouse such fear, until recently occupied a relatively orderly (or in any case, safely contained) place within robust political categories, especially in terms of electoral politics. It occupied a place not beyond some outer margin, but quite close to the centre of our social whole. It was long a factor for stability in the so-called 'Western democracies': notwithstanding the dialectic of political cultures and legitimate interests, it long shared a substantial consensus on the prevalent social model. And it contributed a legitimising role to this model, if only through its passivity.

9

As such, the area on which we need to focus our concerns is not so much the various forms of this protagonist's self-expression, however much we may agree or disagree with them, or the phenomenology of the 'man in revolt' that it offers up to us, but the mechanism of rupture that has produced this metamorphosis. We need to think through the dissolution of these old political containers (the mass parties of the twentieth century, the channels of traditional political participation, the late-industrial forms of aggregation). Along with this 'anthropological' transformation of the masses, in their now-complete transition from producer-consumers to consumers *tout court* (or, to use Benjamin Barber's felicitous expression, 'consumed-consumers')[14] we must reconceptualise the accompanying cultural mutation of the political elites, and the unprecedented rise of their 'herd mentality', precisely as their real autonomy to make decisions has thinned out: a linguistic and behavioural race to the bottom, combined with values that are ever more subaltern . . .

In so doing we would discover – or in any case, this is what I myself experienced as I wrote this book – that what we generically refer to as 'populism' is not a new 'political subject', in the proper sense of the term. But nor is that to say that it is an old one. Populism is not the equivalent of a political party, a movement, an 'actor' with its own structured identity, its own organisational matrix, its own 'political culture' – however subject to hatred or deprecation this culture may be. It is not an 'ism' like the others that we have scattered over the course of modern history, in the manner of socialism, communism, liberalism, fascism and so on, which we either identified with (through

---

14   Benjamin Barber, *Consumed: How Markets Corrupt Children, Infantilize Adults, and Swallow Citizens Whole*, W.W. Norton, New York, 2007.

belonging) or fought against (through opposition). It is a much more impalpable entity, less identifiable within specific confines or labels. It is a mood. It is the formless form that social malaise and impulses to protest take on in societies that have been pulverised and reworked by globalisation and total finance – what Luciano Gallino has called 'finance-capitalism' – in the era in which there is a lack of voice or organisation. Which is to say, in the vacuum produced by the dissolution of what was once 'the Left', and of its capacity to articulate protest as a proposal for change and an alternative to the present state of things.

This demands a focus on what this book defines as a 'populism-as-context'. This constitutes, so to speak, a problematic defined by the 'zeitgeist': the political-cultural climate of our time, which impresses its own changing pattern upon the political life of whole national or even transnational communities. It does so in an all-encompassing way, spanning the whole spectrum of political cultures, influencing their communicative and behavioural styles, establishing codes and forms of rhetoric, forms of argument and modalities of language. Then we will seek to define the other level of populism, what we could consider its – less generic, better-delimited – 'inner circle'. This is what we could define as 'populism-as-project': the populism embodied in a more recognisable 'political subject' endowed with its own 'political culture' and which works not only to give voice to protest, but also to contend for government (and the exercise of power).

2

The Word is Not Enough

We can begin by taking the lead from those who first subjected the category 'populism' to serious study, and term it a 'contested concept'.[1] This term is not only a cudgel to be wielded in the day-to-day political battle, but a fundamentally divisive formula that looms over what ought to be the much more peaceable field of scholarly inquiry. It is a problematic term, which we ought to distrust, keep our distance from, or at least raise a number of questions over. Like those who dedicated themselves to the most complete reflection on populism over half a century ago,[2] we ought to ask ourselves if it is an 'ideology', a 'recurring mentality appearing in different historical and geographic contexts', or even a form of political psychology, or 'anti-phenomenon' (rather, a *people-worshipping phenomenon*, of collective

---

1 See Christa Deiwiks's fine review of this literature, 'Populism', *Living Reviews in Democracy*, June 2009. Its first section is entitled 'A contested concept of populism'.

2 Ionescu and Gellner, *Populism*, which Paul Taggart defined 'The definitive collection on populism' (P. Taggart, *Populism*, Open University Press, Buckingham, PA, 2000).

emotionality). Or finally, 'if populism can be subsumed under nationalism, socialism, and "peasantism"'[3] or deserves a certain autonomy of its own.

Lowest common denominator

The first attempts to arrive at a scientific definition for a 'populism' stipulated an abnormally high number of characteristics. For example, as far back as 1969, Peter Wiles listed some twenty-four characteristics of populism, confirming just how difficult it is to find an even minimal common denominator for such a complicated and heterogeneous phenomenon.[4] Too many, indeed, for them to be of any use at a theoretical level, or applicable on the terrain of empirical analysis. Later, they were more rigorously selected, and ultimately refined to the perfect number of three: that is, what Christa Deiwiks calls populism's core characteristics, as indicated in the 'mature' works defining populism.[5]

The first factor common to all populisms is, naturally, the supreme, paramount centrality assumed therein by the reference to the people, understood in its 'warm' dimension as a living community, almost a sort of pre-political and pre-civic entity, a Rousseauian 'natural state'. An organic entity, which thus does not allow distinctions within its ranks – for they would be seen as damaging and reprehensible divisions. This also grounds a

---

3   Deiwiks, 'Populism', p. 1.

4   Peter Wiles, 'A Syndrome, Not a Doctrine: Some Elementary Theses on Populism', in Ionescu and Gellner, *Populism*.

5   Like that edited by two authoritative French political scientists: see Yves Mény and Yves Surel (eds.), *Democracies and the Populist Challenge*, Palgrave Macmillan, New York, 2002.

particular conception of political conflict: no longer the traditional, 'horizontal' dialectic between the different political cultures in which citizenship articulates itself, of which the Left–Right couple is the richest example. Here, instead, we have the 'vertical' distinction – or rather, counterposition – between the whole people in its uncontaminated original purity, and some other entity that unduly stands above it (a usurping elite, a privileged gang, a hidden power) or insinuates itself from below (immigrants, foreigners, travellers). In any case, there must be some 'extraneous' and 'hostile' element whose own presence as the negative pole in the new political dialectic brings into relief the 'true' people and confirms its unity. And moreover, in assuming this new type of counterposition as itself constitutive of 'the Political' (as an essential form of what Carl Schmitt called the 'friend–enemy' pairing),[6] it drives a ninety-degree turn in the spatial framework of political conflict. For it marks the shift from the horizontal spatiality typical of the modernity that began with the French Revolution – in which (at least at the level of political conflict among citizens) the contending protagonists stood on the same footing of equality, different in ideas but not in rank – to a vertical one in which the logic of 'above and below' instead prevails. Indeed, in this spatiality, the protagonists in the conflict belong to different levels and, in some senses, opposed and self-referential life-worlds.

The second factor they have in common has something to do, directly or indirectly, with the idea of betrayal: with some abuse, some undue misappropriation, some conspiracy organised at the expense of the honest citizens. This conforms to a style of

---

6   Carl Schmitt, *The Concept of the Political*, Expanded Edition (1932), trans. by G. Schwab, University of Chicago Press, Chicago, 2007, p. 26.

thinking that reframes conflict not only in political or social terms but also, primarily, in ethical' ones: as the moral counterposition of the righteous and the ungodly, the honest and the corrupt, 'ours' and 'theirs' . . . Hence every form of populism is more or less fundamentally connected to some moral construction of the antithetical 'other', in the conflict in which the constitutive values of the community of reference are ultimately revealed. In turn, this community can itself be taken as a 'heartland' – the protective shelter within whose confines the single individuals whose identity is threatened can find some collective comfort. And, conversely, we can say that the 'people' in any populism is a narrative construction: it is the product of a 'narrative', or, as Ernesto Laclau argues,[7] the discursive creation of an 'empty signifier' around which 'the Political' structures itself, in which the heterogeneous society can see an undifferentiated reflection of itself.

The last factor they have in common has to do with the imaginary of upheaval: chasing out the usurper-oligarchy – i.e., removing the 'foreign body' – and restoring a popular sovereignty that is finally recognised. This sovereignty is no longer exercised through the mediation of the old representative institutions, but thanks to the action of the leader (who tends to be a charismatic leader or in any case emotionally linked to 'ordinary folks' [la gente] by way of transferral mechanisms), and able to act 'for the good of the people', or, as they claim, to guarantee the 'public well-being'. This explains why populisms generally assume a 'revolutionary' language and style, and in some cases even a visionary or prophetic (chiliastic) one, without this meaning that they necessary mount any radical challenge to the social

---

7   Ernesto Laclau, *On Populist Reason*, Verso Books, New York, 2005.

order or property ownership. In fact, they often limit the radical dimension of change to the level of government personnel alone. At the same time, this sheds light on the reasons why, for populism to be able to take root and grow, there must exist some anomalous context. It needs some particular conjuncture marked by the faultlines of deep crisis (an 'extreme' crisis, it is suggested) in the established order, institutions and their political personnel, as well as a widespread and generally virulent malaise which translates into a pervasive process of delegitimation and distrust toward any ruling class (any elite) identifiable with the present state of things.

'Above/below' versus 'Right/Left'

To arrive at a synthetic formula, we can embrace the one provided by the Dutch political scientist Cas Mudde at the beginning of the 2000s, when he defined populism as 'an ideology that considers society to be ultimately separated into two homogeneous and antagonistic groups, "the pure people" versus "the corrupt elite", and which argues that politics should be an expression of the *volonté générale* (general will) of the people'.[8] A few years before that, another scholar, the American Michael Kazin,[9] considered populism 'not an ideology [but] an impulse' and also a 'form of expression'. It is thus above all a 'political style', a 'form' rather than a set of contents. But he reached the same conclusions as Mudde as regards the fundamental 'bipolar' or 'bifocal' characteristic of the 'populist syndrome': that is, the determination to

---

8 Cas Mudde, 'The Populist Zeitgeist', in *Government and Opposition*, 2004, p. 543.
9 Kazin, *The Populist Persuasion*.

17

divide the political space into 'above and below', in the counter-position between '*the powerful and the powerless*':

> The haughty financier wraps chains of debt around small farmers who grow food and fibers for the nation. The stout industrialist – top hat on his fleshy head and diamond stick-pin gleaming from his silk tie – clashes with the working man dressed in overalls or secondhand suit, his jaw firm and his muscles taut. The federal bureaucrat, overeducated and amoral, scoffs at the God-fearing nuclear family in its modest home, a crucifix on the wall and a flagpole in the yard.[10]

Simplifying things, we could say that almost all the definitions in the main dictionaries will settle on this 'format', so to speak, such as the entry for 'populist' in the *Merriam-Webster Dictionary*, which reads: 'a member of a political party claiming to represent the common people' or the *Cambridge Dictionary*, which describes 'populism' as 'political ideas and activities that are intended to get the support of ordinary people by giving them what they want' and also 'the political doctrine that supports the rights and powers of the common people in their struggle with the privileged elite'. Or the *Business Dictionary*, which offers a rather more developed version: 'In general, ideology or political movement that mobilizes the population (often, but not always, the lower classes) against an institution or government, usually in the defense of the underdog or the wronged.' This relatively widespread common ground would seem to confirm our impression that, by the end of the twentieth century, populism – which had doubtless been a

---

10   Ibid., p. 1.

protagonist of that century, always lurking behind its fierce ideo-logical and social clashes – had now 'stabilised' as a phenomenon: it had been well-established at the theoretical level. And, indeed, it was a phenomenon that had been confined to the geographical margins, in terms of where it was an insurgent political force: South America, of course, and perhaps also in the former provinces of the Soviet Empire after its collapse. Meanwhile at the centre – in the heart of the reinforced West – it could be considered a fire that had now gone out, suffocated in largely anaemic, passive and tired democracies which had now been emptied of their passions and stabilised through their lack of alternatives.

Anti-politics

But no. The following decade – the one in which the profile of the new century took shape – has seen the populist challenge coming back in a big way. Exemplary, from this point of view, was a recent debate in the pages of the *Guardian*[11], a paper that can hardly be suspected of being over-emotional or raising scandals. The debate began with a cry of alarm – 'The populists are coming!' and continued in worried tones: 'In many European countries, so-called "populist" political parties are on the rise, disrupting the established political order and upstaging main-stream parties'. This was an anomalous challenge, on account of its spatial location (the peripheries of the centre rather than the centres of the peripheries, as before); its mass protagonists (the 'middling' social strata, the great belly of mature societies that are

---

11   In the 'Debating Europe' section, with the title 'Why is "populism" seen as such a bad thing?', started 15 February 2016 (with interviews of Cas Mudde and Paul Taggart).

now losing their class position); and the dark ills it revealed. This was no longer a matter of pointing to specific aspects of political life and the institutional order, but of politics as such: its alienness to citizens' *lives*, and its inability to read their needs and feelings and to respond to their essential demands. This was a sort of great exodus which – like many great fractures – also brought forth new words.

The first of them was 'anti-politics'. This word is ambiguous, just like the emotion that drives it, namely the panic of the various establishment forces at the sudden challenge it presented to them. From a lexical point of view, this term is hardly new. Rather, it must have a long history, if already in the 1940s the historian Luigi Salvatorelli criticised Guglielmo Giannini and his Uomo qualunque movement for recycling 'the old [*sic!*] twaddle of anti-politics'.[12] But it long remained confined to the specialist discourse from which it emerged in the seventeenth century, together with the appearance of the category of 'politics' as an autonomous sphere, fundamental to and constitutive of the 'social'. It emerged by way of antithesis, through the practice of qualifying with a pejorative 'anti' any conception of politics that did not conform to the opinion of the author.[13] It then returned, at the height of the century,[14] in the dispute between political philosophers over Carl Schmitt's theological-reactionary idea that the categories of the

---

12   As mentioned by Franco Di Lonardo, *L'antipolitica come problema: teoria e riferimenti empirici*, Political Science laureate dissertation, Università del Piemonte Orientale Amedeo Avogadro, Alessandria, 1997.

13   Carlo Galli, 'Antipolitica', in the 'La parola' section, Repubblica.it, 4 November 2012.

14   Pier Paolo Portinaro, 'Antipolitica o fine della politica? Considerazioni sul presente disorientamento teorico', *Teoria politica*, IV, 1988.

political had been 'neutralised' (the 'end of politics' as a secularised theology) by liberal juridical technocracy, and, opposed to this, Hannah Arendt's critique 'of the reduction of politics to the phenomenon of power' by modern science, and the consequent liquidation of the ethical-communicative dimension it had in ancient philosophy.[15] But this was, indeed, a dispute among scholars. It would take until the end of the century for the word 'anti-politics' to break out of these limits and come to prominence in the vernacular. In 1992, its German version – the term *Politikverdrossenheit* – was proclaimed the 'word of the year' by the *Gesellschaft für deutsche Sprache* in recognition of its spread across the press and in political debate, followed in turn by *Fremdemhass* (xenophobia) and *Rassismus* (racism). And from then on, its use has continued to proliferate.

At first, the term still had rather a passive connotation: it alluded to a sort of tiredness (among the electorate), a distance or coldness toward politics: indeed, in German, *Verdrossenheit* means 'apathy', 'reluctance'. It described the process that was now underway in well-ordered Germany, in which a growing mass of disappointed voters abandoned the parties, both as a whole and particularly the two main ones, most central to the stability of the political system. This was what political scientists would call an 'exit', an exodus, but not yet a 'voice', in the proper sense of a protest. But, subsequently, the level of aggression which the term expressed would increase, and it was further applied to multiple forms of protest and genuine electoral revolt: to the birth of antagonistic movements and the rise of increasingly successful new political formations (ones, in general, reluctant to define themselves using the category 'party').

---

15   Ibid., p. 122.

It was then that the word 'anti-politics' began to be used en masse, in public discourse, as synonymous with 'populism'. But this was an improper use of language. It was a fraudulent lexical operation, largely deployed by the mainstream webs of journalism. It was telling of the sense of unease – if not actual fear – among establishment political forces, so cloistered in their own self-identification with the 'monopoly on politics' that they considered the emergence of any alternative to themselves as nothing more than a 'negation of politics', and, indeed, an 'anti-politics'. This is obviously nonsense, for as Aristotle showed in the domain of philosophy, whoever wants to do without philosophy is compelled to make a philosophical argument for that; similarly, the most radical or even extreme opposition to politics inevitably ends up expressing itself politically. This truth was illustrated once more in a chapter of Thomas Mann's *Reflections of a Nonpolitical Man*, written in the dark heart of the twentieth century, at the very moment that politics began fully to reveal its own 'demonic face'. This chapter would seem to be on a quite different subject, being titled 'On Virtue'. But it began with a striking methodological note: 'To speak of the opposite of a matter is also a way of speaking of the matter itself – even a way in which objective understanding is admirably served.'[16] It continues: 'But antipolitics is also politics, for politics is a terrible force: If one only knows about it, one has already succumbed to it. One has lost one's innocence.'[17]

---

16   Thomas Mann, *Reflections of an Nonpolitical Man*, trans. by Walter D. Morris, Ungar, New York, 1987, p. 273.

17   Ibid., p. 303.

The new populism

After the shock (but not the fear) had subsided, there was a return to more appropriate terms; the prefix 'new' before the term 'populism' now became increasingly commonplace. This was especially true of the US press, as it sought to label the various insurgent forces appearing in the wake of Occupy Wall Street and the consequent emergence in the collective imaginary of the 99 per cent of the population counterposed to the privileged 1 per cent. The followers of organisations like the Campaign for America's Future[18] – part advocacy association, part think tank, on the left wing of the Democratic Party – were called 'new populists' and indeed described themselves using this term. This organisation had the objective of 'mobiliz[ing] the Democratic base – unions, African Americans, Hispanics, women, environmentalists – while reaching out to seniors and working families'. In the 2008 presidential elections it supported Barack Obama against Hillary Clinton, and in 2014 its annual meet-up in Washington took the title 'The New Populism Conference'. Democratic senator Elizabeth Warren was chosen to make the opening speech; her oration sermonised:

We believe no one should work full-time and live in poverty, and that means raising the minimum wage – and we're

---

18   It was founded as a 'strategic centre for the progressive movement', as its instrument of incorporation tells us, by Robert Borosage, a lawyer, scholar of questions of law, politics and international relations, and director of the Institute for Policy Studies, and Roger Hickey, founder of the Economic Policy Institute and promoter of the campaign against the privatisation of Social Security. It had the aim of counterbalancing the weight exercised within the Democratic Party by the moderate Democratic Leadership Council.

willing to fight for it. We believe people should retire with dignity, and that means strengthening Social Security – and we're willing to fight for it. We believe that a kid should have a chance to go to college without getting crushed by debt – and we're willing to fight for it. We believe workers have a right to come together, to bargain together and to rebuild America's middle class – and we're willing to fight for it. We believe in equal pay for equal work – and we're willing to fight for it. We believe equal means equal, and that's true in the workplace and in marriage, true for all our families – and we're winning that fight right now. We – the people – decide the future of this country. These are our shared values. And we are willing to fight for them. This is our fight![19]

Later, in 2016, the Campaign would back Bernie Sanders in the Democratic primaries.

Yet, on the opposite side, the variegated galaxy of Tea Parties would also fall under this same term. Indeed, a detailed 2011 study on them by Political Research Associates – a think tank that occupies a similar political space to the Campaign for America's Future – was entitled 'The Tea Party: the New Populism'.[20] It dated the Tea Party's emergence to a few years before, in February 2009, when a CNBC pundit – Rick Santelli, a financial analyst of Italian-American origin – launched into a particularly severe rebuke of the newly elected president Barack Obama, who

---

19   Elizabeth Warren, 'Speech at The New Populism Conference in Washington', 22 May 2014.

20   Arun Gupta, *The Tea Party: The new populism*, Political Research Associates, 1 August 2011.

had two days previously decided to allocate $787bn to support the economy devastated by the sub-prime crisis and another $75bn in direct aid to homeowners to help them refinance their mortgages. In this speech Santelli excoriated the government, accusing it of encouraging 'bad behavior . . . subsidiz[ing] the losers' mortgages' and failing to 'reward people that can carry the water instead of drink the water'.[21] 'This is America!', Santelli proclaimed – the silent majority, white, hardworking, made up of shopkeepers, businessmen, investors who did not want to depend on the government. And he set the date for a 'Chicago Tea Party', thus opening Pandora's Box . . .

Obviously, this speech was the polar opposite to Warren's, for it was directed at dividing people from their peers rather than uniting them with others who were different from them: 'How many of you people want to pay for your neighbor's mortgage that has an extra bathroom and can't pay their bills', Santelli hissed. A discourse that nonetheless – or better, precisely for this reason – had an enormous contagious force (and now the 'rant' began to be 'heard round the world', as the title of the report's first chapter put it).[22] It won ever more ground among Republican voters – and to a lesser extent, among the party's representatives – much like the effect the discourse of the Campaign for America's Future had among Democratic ranks. This is a dynamic relatively unprecedented in the history of the mature democracies, in which more radical political cultures tend to give rise to organisationally autonomous formations. Indeed, this dynamic is also without precedent in the history of the classic populisms, or the twentieth-century ones at least. For in assuming characteristics

---

21   Ibid., p. 1
22   'The Rant Heard Round the World', in ibid.

that were anti-systemic in tendency, or manifestly so, they formed completely separate structures and took on political identities that could not be mediated. But now on opposite ends of the political system – on the Left as on the Right – we can see the near-simultaneous emergence of this same phenomenon; what we might call the 'contamination' of their respective electoral bases and supporters by populist 'styles'. And we can well understand the perplexity with which 'progressives' looked on at the first emergence of the Tea Parties, as they were wrong-footed by the 'mass movement from below' that seemed to be 'marching to the tune of well-funded, top-down organizations and prominent right-wing media'[23] with an unprecedented message of revolt. But it was precisely this sense of novelty – a genuine split with the past – that justified the label 'new' being applied to all the various emerging forms of populism.

Populism revisited

Lastly, the most recent analyses, following the social and political upheavals produced by the Great Recession, are marked by a more attentive consideration of the difference between 'populism as context' and 'populism as project' to which we referred at the end of the previous chapter. That is, between populism as a generic (and generalised) mood – attached to a still-vague attitude of distance from, and hostility toward, institutional actors and the establishment – and, on the other hand, populism as a true and proper political culture unto itself, determined to seek power in a strategic manner, on the basis of a specific political programme. With this second, less generic sense of populism,

---

23   Ibid., Second Chapter, p. 2.

awareness has grown of the sharp divergence in the various 'souls' of this phenomenon. Or, if you prefer, between 'political families' that are so distant from one another (and essentially, counterposed) that they can no longer be brought together under the same term.

Very telling, in this sense, is the approach taken by John B. Judis. In his *The Populist Explosion*, he explicitly proposes to take Kazin's characterisation 'one step further' and draw a sharp distinction between a 'left-wing populism' (like that of Sanders, Tsipras and Iglesias) and a 'right-wing populism' (like that of Trump, Le Pen and Orbán). This, not only because they differ in terms of their respective targets (the type of policies they are proposing) but also – and above all – because they are characterised by a different ordering of political conflict. 'Left-wing populists', Judis writes 'champion the people against an elite or an establishment. Theirs is a vertical politics of the bottom and middle arrayed against the top.' Conversely, 'rightwing populists champion the people against an elite that they accuse of coddling a third group, which can consist, for instance, of immigrants, Islamists, or African American militants.' The first type – left-wing populism' has a 'dyadic' structure, whereas right-wing populism has a 'triadic' structure: 'It looks upward, but also down upon an out group.'[24] The first, we could add, follows the schema of a classic social conflict (even if 'it is not a politics of class conflict, and it doesn't necessarily seek the abolition of capitalism').[25] In the second, there comes into play the atypical

---

24   John B. Judis, *The Populist Explosion. How the Great Recession Transformed American and European Politics*, Columbia Global Reports, New York, 2016.

25   Ibid.

figure of the scapegoat (what has been called 'this demagoguing of the scapegoat du jour')[26] which splits the level of conflict into two by adding a second plane of antagonism with a 'weaker' protagonist who is nonetheless accused of enjoying undue privileges.

Jan-Werner Müller also alludes to a substantial difference between the various meanings of the term 'populism', though he does so more indirectly, and in greater consonance with Mudde and Kazin's schemas. The first and most generic of these meanings – the critique of governing oligarchies – is today so diffuse and widely shared that it cannot be given a political characterisation, in the strict sense ('Not everyone who criticises elites is a populist'). At the same time, Müller acknowledges that it is in fact impossible to draw a comparison between the different 'left-wing' and 'right-wing' 'families' of populism, as if they made up one political culture. When, in the second of his *Seven Theses on Populism*, he states that 'in addition to being antielitist, populists are antipluralist'[27] he refers to a characteristic element of this phenomenon that in fact only applies to the 'family of the Right': to that component which, in Judis's reading, constructs the unity of the people conceived 'as a whole' using techniques that are particularly dear to organicist and, in general, nationalist political cultures. These latter tend to favour an ethnic, racial or in any case strongly identitarian connotation of 'people' and its ring-fencing or 'spatialisation' within societies that are enclosed behind strongly drawn borders and boundaries. This connotation does apply to political phenomena like Trump in the United

---

26   Jonathan Alter, '"The Populist Explosion" Dissects the History of the Anti-Elite Worldview', *The New York Times*, 7 October 2016.

27   Müller, *What Is Populism?*, p. 101.

States; Orbán in Hungary and the political formations on the rise in the Visegrad region more generally; Marine Le Pen in France; Matteo Salvini in Italy; and the AfD in Germany – but certainly not to movements like Podemos in Spain or Syriza in Greece. This book will focus especially on this former group, those in which what we have called 'populism-as-project' is most evident.

Then there is another element, common to both Judis and Müller, which has become ever more obvious over the last five years, marked by the 'work' the Great Recession has done to the social and political body of the West. It introduces something of an innovation in the populist phenomenon, characteristic of what we might call the 'populism of the new millennium' and which marks its difference from its twentieth-century predecessors; namely, its 'genetic' relationship with an unprecedented systemic crisis. This is a crisis of representation and, at the same time, a crisis of the legitimation of contemporary political systems, which have suddenly been left without any ideology to justify them. They seem incapable of keeping faith with their own promises or remaining true to the fundamentals that convinced their respective citizenries to trust in their mechanisms of government, beginning with the first foundation of 'democratic government': popular sovereignty.

Judis articulates this very clearly, when he writes that populist parties and movements become successful 'only under certain circumstances'. Which is to say, in 'times when people see the prevailing political norms – put forward, preserved and defended by the leading segments in the country – as being at odds with their own hopes, fears, and concerns'.[28] When they experience the existing political order as something radically hostile, and, in

---

28 Judis, *The Populist Explosion*, pp. 120–6.

many aspects, intolerable and alien to them. Such are the ingredients of a real political crisis that is also a 'systemic crisis', in which the 'neglected concerns' of what may even be a majority of the population point to the seizing up of the mechanisms of democratic representation and the emergence of a systemic deficit of legitimacy (in this sense, the populists 'signal that . . . the standard worldview is breaking down').[29] Müller asserts this similarly forcefully when he connects the 'anger' that constitutes the main fuel of the present populist wave (especially in the United States) with a 'sense that the country is changing culturally in ways deeply objectionable to a certain percentage of American citizens'.[30] Above all, he identifies as the crucial factor in the present populist syndrome the widespread feeling that the sacred principle of 'popular sovereignty' has been betrayed by liberal elites. He turns to Benjamin Arditi's fable of the 'awkward guest', which compares the populist to 'the drunken guest at a dinner party: he is not respecting table manners, he is rude, he might even start "flirting with the wives of other guests" '. But he might also be blurting out the truth about a liberal democracy that has become forgetful about its founding ideal of popular sovereignty'.[31]

Arditi – one of the most brilliant analysts of contemporary populism – uses this metaphor of the 'awkward guest' in an essay rich in cues for reflection, his 'Populism as an Internal Periphery

---

29   Ibid.

30   He refers here to the 'increasing influence of, broadly speaking, social-sexual liberal values (same-sex marriage, etc.) and also concerns about the United States becoming a "majority-minority country," in which traditional images of "the real people" – white Protestants, that is – have less and less purchase on social reality': Müller, *What is Populism?*, p. 91.

31   Ibid., p. 8.

of Democratic Politics'.[32] And he uses it precisely to illustrate the thesis that present-day populism is symptomatic of a structural crisis of democratic politics, which has become incapable of keeping its people in its proper place (i.e. within the 'normalised space' of politics) at a time in which the 'place assigned to them' no longer suits enough people, or the 'place of the excluded underdog' has become unacceptable to them.[33] Populism would then be – to use this author's words – a 'paradoxical element', 'within' democracy, endorsing its formal aspects ('the public debate of political issues, electoral participation, informal forms of expression of the popular will, and so on') and, at the same time, 'interrupts its closure as a domesticated political order' caged within 'the institutions, normative codes, practices, procedures and rituals that are part of our political normality').[34] It is a 'noise' or a 'disturbance' that signals a process of dis-identification between the *demos* and *kratos* [power] such as it is exercised. This process is, in turn, symmetrical and counterposed to a parallel separation process (of 'missing recognition') between the *kratos* (of the governing oligarchy and its institutions, ever more impermeable to what comes from below) and the *demos* and its 'sufferings'. The tensions and factors behind the conflict that had been silenced and relegated to this 'inner foreign land' (as Freud termed the unconscious) now tend to break out and emerge into the light, precisely by means of this crack in the only apparently hard surface of a pacified post-democracy. Their disorderly arrival on the scene tends to

---

32   Benjamin Arditi, 'Populism as an Internal Periphery of Democratic Politics', *Politics on the Edges of Liberalism*, Edinburgh University Press, Edinburgh, 2007, pp. 54–87.

33   Ibid., pp. 78–9.

34   Ibid., p. 77.

interrupt the perpetual peace of the 'age of neutralisations' (as Carl Schmitt defined political modernity centred on the administrative state and government reduced to technocracy) and returns to the field the fatal 'friend–enemy' pairing that embodies the very essence of 'the Political'. According to this perspective, it would seem, populism should not be confused with anti-politics or the apolitical, but instead proves to be a form of hyper-politics, without precedent at least since World War II. Or, to adopt Laclau's expression, it is the form that politics assumes today, at the end of the long cycle of 'democratic normalisation'.

The Italian case: neo-populism in struggle and in government

This much is true for the Anglosphere. But this terminology has also undergone a certain shift in Europe, with a clear discontinuity in the dictionary definition. This is especially the case in Italy, which, in the first part of this century, has become a genuine collective laboratory for all the various types of populism.

The entry for *populismo* in the updated 2016 edition of Italy's most authoritative political dictionary – the *Dizionario di politica* edited by Norberto Bobbio, Nicola Matteucci and Gianfranco Pasquino[35] – has a final paragraph, separated from the entry itself, with its own autonomous title: *il neopopulismo*.[36] Indeed, here it is

---

35 Norberto Bobbio, Nicola Matteucci, Gianfranco Pasquino (eds.), *Dizionario di Politica*, new updated edition, UTET, Novara 2016.

36 The entry 'Populismo' written by Ludovico Incisa di Camerana, which was also included in previous editions, has been expanded through the addition of a new seventh paragraph, 'Neopopulismo', by Davide Grassi, p. 737.

observed that, unlike the classic forms assumed by what we might call 'first generation' populism, generally inspired by some form of nationalism and in part by statism, post-twentieth century populism appears – at least to a significant degree – in close connection with the neoliberal wave that characterised the turn of the century. Indeed, it draws rhetorical and programmatic assonances and inclinations from this wave. It incorporates some of its precepts, transferring them to the macro-economic and social level onto the plane of its own political projects. We see this, for example, in the appeal the neo-populists direct in particular toward un-organised and often strongly individualist sectors of society that are not identifiable with the traditional social blocs. Indeed, while classical populism 'encouraged forms of social mobilisation through the creation of organisations of interests', neo-populism tends to 'overstep the existing organisations' and in some regards to pull them apart or in any case delegitimise them, in the attempt – shared by the neoliberal credo – 'of undoing the positions of privilege acquired by certain interest groups within civil society and the economy'.[37]

We can think, here, of Beppe Grillo's original project for the Five Star Movement and the polemics it directed against the trade union movement, professional associations, the journalists' union etc. But so, too, of the conservative revolution attempted by Matteo Renzi as secretary of the Democratic Party and as head of government, and the campaign he waged against 'intermediate bodies' and the traditional forms of social representation, in the name of 'packing them off to the junk yard' (the famous *rottamazione*). As we read in this extra paragraph to the entry in the *Dizionario*,

---

37 Ibid.

Against trade unions' parasitic rent income, business cartels, bureaucrats and 'career politicians', the neo-populist response would [supposedly, at least] guarantee the interests of marginalised or excluded sectors of society and 'ordinary people', and like the neoliberal response would guarantee opportunities for the economic affirmation of peripheral layers, new entrepreneurs and 'outsiders'.[38]

The same applies to the institutional order and form of government. 'The strengthening of the executive at the expense of parliament and parties represents a point the two doctrines [neoliberalism and neopopulism] have in common', the text continues: 'Imposing reforms from above without bending to compromises and deals with different political and social groups will help defeat the resistance of establishment interests and facilitate the necessary structural reforms of the economy'.[39] (And, we might add, these are the same reforms so urgently demanded by the great extra-institutional powers of the neoliberal order, from the global investment banks to the International Monetary Fund and the European Central Bank). Here, the new part of the entry on 'populismo' seems imbued with the trace of the Italian events connected with Matteo Renzi's rise to office and his rhetoric of the 'scrapper' and the country 'changing direction' – in addition, of course, to the style in which he launched and promoted the constitutional reform named after himself and his minister Maria Elena Boschi (defeated by referendum in December 2016). Here were 'political outsiders' committed to presenting themselves as something new, free from ties to the old

---

38 Ibid.
39 Ibid.

power structures and thus – it could be presupposed – able to realise the institutional innovations that the markets demanded. This ultimately provides an example of a 'neopopulism' understood as a 'populism from above' or a 'populism of government', thus constituting a further variant of this model. And it would seem to have found its happiest hunting-ground in Italy.

Looking more directly at the level of political activism, it is particularly telling to note the emergence and gradual spread, especially in Italy, of a literature that is radically critical of the institutional order, and which tends to locate the populist emergency (or 'outpouring') in the context of the epochal rupture of the end of the twentieth century. This was a rupture marked by globalisation, the new socio-productive paradigm that came with the end of 'Fordism', the emergence of new technologies and the totalisation of the mass-media sphere, and above all the social defeat of 'labour' and the dissolution of the twentieth-century labour movement. At the same time, it is interesting to note that, while their authors come from a left-wing or far-left milieu, a considerable part of these analyses tends to converge around 'sovereigntyist' or 'neo-sovereigntyist' positions. Carlo Formenti's book *La variante populista* is notably indicative of this phenomenon.[40]

In this volume, the emergence of the 'latest generation of populism', which has now stably occupied the political field in the West, is situated in close causal connection with the historic defeat that 'labour' suffered, on the global scale, at the end of the twentieth century, and the catastrophic abandonment of the popular classes by their own political representatives, as

---

40 Carlo Formenti, *La variante populista. Lotta di classe nel neoliberismo*, DeriveApprodi, Roma, 2016.

embodied by the twentieth-century Left. For Formenti, 'The class war from above that capital has waged in recent decades has been so effective that not only has it managed to strangle the resistance of the subordinate classes: it has modified . . . their very anthropology'. And he adds: 'those political forces that, for their own unfathomable reasons, continue to call themselves left-wing . . . have not just adapted to the socio-political and cultural context generated by the capitalist offensive, but they actively contribute to its reproduction'.[41] According to the author, faced with these left-wing cultures that now belong to a different part of society and use the term 'populist' as an insult, we ought to reply with Naulot's cutting remark: 'Populist: an adjective the Left uses to designate the people when they start to abandon it.'[42]

From this perspective, we could say that,

for Formenti as for Laclau, populism is the general form that politics assumes in the present, even if the former's approach is apparently counterposed to the latter's 'linguistic constructivism'. The categories of Formenti's analysis are in fact oriented toward a substantialism that sees not discourse but the concrete operation of neoliberal ideological and practical mechanisms as the means of producing social subjects and identifies the terms of the new configuration of the 'enemy-friend' pairing in the – ever so material – conflict between (global) circulation and (territorially-rooted) places. The enemy is 'the ' "immaterial" and "light" world of circulation (of commodities, of services, of symbols

---

41   Ibid., p. 255.

42   Jean-Claude Guillebaud, 'Populisme', *Décodeur de la pensée unique*, in *Respublica*, April 1996, p. 96.

of value, of information and of the members of the governing elites)' – which are, in reality, highly 'material' and very 'heavy' – frontally opposed to 'the world of the places where the bodies that want food, housing, work and emotional wellbeing live'. And, for this reason, 'accepting the challenge of populism means understanding that it is impossible to oppose global capital without fighting to win back popular sovereignty, which in turn involves winning back national sovereignty'.[43]

---

43   Ibid.

3

From the Origins to the Apprentice

The original populists

We meet in the midst of a nation brought to the verge of
moral, political, and material ruin. Corruption dominates
the ballot-box, the Legislatures, the Congress, and touches
even the ermine of the bench. The people are demoral-
ized . . . The newspapers are largely subsidized or muzzled,
public opinion silenced, business prostrated, homes covered
with mortgages, labor impoverished, and the land concen-
trating in the hands of capitalists . . . A vast conspiracy
against mankind has been organized on two continents, and
it is rapidly taking possession of the world.[1]

These words were not the rallying cry at some rally for the Bernie
Sanders campaign, back in the spring of 2016 when he still seemed
in with a chance of winning the Democratic primaries. Nor were
they a rhetorical flourish at one of Donald Trump's final events
that October, as he made his last push in the apparently desperate

---

1   Michael Kazin, *The Populist Persuasion*, p. 28.

effort to scrape together the votes of the forgotten poor of the Midwest and thus keep pace with Hillary Clinton or even beat her in the race to the White House. Rather, the text quoted above is the preamble to the grandiose statement that gave rise to the National People's Party (also known as the Populist Party) on 4 July 1892, – the so-called Omaha Platform. However ephemeral this party, it was the most fully realised and organised form ever taken by 'classical' American populism – what Michael Kazin defines as the original populists.

The text of this 'seminal' document was written by Ignatius Donnelly, a versatile personality from Minnesota. A Roman Catholic of Irish origins and a lawyer by profession, as well as an amateur researcher (and author of bizarre theories on Atlantis and on Shakespeare, whose works he attributed to Francis Bacon), Donnelly was a politician involved first in the radical wing of the Republican Party (taking up a post as vice-governor) and then in the nascent Populist Party.[2] To him is owed the statement that 'Jesus was only possible in a barefoot world, and he was crucified by the few who wore shoes', as well as incontrovertible assertions in the Platform like the one sermonising that 'If any will not work neither shall he eat'. He had already anticipated the public delivery of the Platform a few months earlier, in a 22 February 1892 speech – the anniversary of George Washington's birth – in the great St Louis Exposition Hall, where the new party's formation process was officially set in motion.

A vast crowd of delegates assembled in that hall, convinced of the party's project: as the reporter for Joseph Pulitzer's famous

---

2   On Donnelly's political career see John D. Hicks's article, 'The political career of Ignatius Donnelly', *The Mississippi Valley Historical Review*, VIII, 2013.

Post-Dispatch 'sympathetically' noted, each of them was a 'history maker'.[3] It was a heterogeneous crowd, whose key base was the mass of 'debt-ridden small farmers in cotton-growing regions of the old Confederacy and wheat-growing areas of the Great Plains'.[4] But it was also joined by many representatives of the middle class, the 'anti-saloon crusaders', the AFL, as well as the Christian socialists of the evangelical churches, and the scattered forces that drove a wide array of radical reformatories organised in myriad clubs.

What brought them together was a diffuse discontent – or, rather, a real anger, born of disappointment – toward both the Democrat and Republican parties. This anger owed to these parties' patronage, their open transgression of democratic rules, and the oligarchic co-optation and corruption of their apparatuses, in flagrant violation of the implicit promises of the American democracy born of the revolution. This was compounded by the indignation felt at the growing inequalities in a society that was seeing the emergence of the first monopolies, as well as the vast fortunes accumulated by the big bankers and the rail bosses, even as the country's productive soul hung in the balance. This was all summarised in the central theme of the struggle against 'an elite whose power appeared both monstrous and seamless',[5] propagated by an array of 'plebeian preachers and secular propagandists' through a rhetoric that mixed the pious creed of the Protestant Reformation ('the belief in a personal God unmediated through spiritual authority')[6] and the

---

3   *St. Louis Post-Dispatch*, 22 February 1892.
4   Kazin, *The Populist Persuasion*, p. 27.
5   Ibid., p. 28.
6   Ibid., p. 10.

Enlightenment philosophy which held that 'ordinary people could think and act rationally, more rationally, in fact, than their ancestral overlords.'[7]

Roots

This phenomenon had deep roots. Indeed, in the clear and simple prose of the Omaha Platform, it is possible to detect the sporadic re-surfacing of the great foundational themes peculiar to the democracy of the 'New World', starting with the radically democratic individualism that Thomas Jefferson had introduced in the 1776 Declaration of Independence (he wrote the famous passage according to which 'We hold . . . that all men are created equal, that they are endowed by their Creator with certain unalienable Rights, that among these are Life, Liberty and the pursuit of Happiness'. And then the 'patriotic productivism' of Andrew Jackson, the seventh US president and the first of humble origins (as a young man he was a saddler's apprentice). He was also the first to have a nickname, 'Old Hickory', and he ushered in 'the age of common man' (the 1830s–40s), also introducing a plebeian and popular – or rather, folk – style of expression made up of sharp and sometimes even rough (or for his critics, crude) manners and a directness of language that had certainly not been seen before. His 'blunt words and acts' were effective enough to encourage his enthusiastic supporters to treat him as 'the fighting . . . man who would save the republic from its enemies'[8] (itself showing the many overlapping ties between republicanism

---

7   Ibid., p. 11.

8   Marvin Meyers, *The Jacksonian Persuasion: Politics and Belief*, Stanford University Press, Stanford, CA, 1957, p. 4.

and an existential populism). This language was a tool to 'mobilize the forces of Democracy against the aristocratic "money power" of his day',[9] introducing into the political lexicon expressions destined to become commonplaces of populist rhetoric, including 'monster banks' and 'financial monopolies' – terms that are still used even today. These 'enemies' were counterposed against a vigorous defence of those who toiled 'with hammer and hand', 'the industrious part of the community'[10] and the ethic of manual labour characterised as 'the only authentic, honest and natural' kind.

With his 'Jacksonian' model of democracy, Andrew Jackson can be considered not only the founder of the Democratic Party (breaking from the Democratic-Republican Party) but also the first American populist in the proper sense of the word (not for nothing he assumed as a second nickname 'King Mob').

We could add that this populist transition was accompanied by a cultural turn whose notes would again be heard half a century later, amidst a further social, economic and, in many regards, anthropological transformation – that which took place between the 1880s and 1890s – in the words and actions of other key figures in US populism. These included such notable figures as Thomas Watson – perhaps the most visible leader of the People's Party – or James Weaver – Populist candidate at the 1892 presidential election, in which he achieved a remarkable, if temporary, success.

---

9   Kazin, *The Populist Persuasion*, p. 18.
10   On this, see G. McKenna, *American Populism*, pp. 69–70; and Kazin, *The Populist Persuasion*, p. 13.

The core of American populism . . .

Thomas Watson (born in Georgia) was a typical Southern radical-democratic activist. He was a teacher and then a jurist (he practised as a barrister), journalist and writer. He was a fierce critic of the political and moral degradation of the Republican Party from the years immediately following the War of Succession, accusing it of being full of corrupt 'boodlers' as well as 'monopolists, gamblers, gigantic corporations, bondholders, bankers'.[11] For long years, he was active in the Democratic Party, to which he brought the 'agrarian' perspective of the farmers and small proprietors of the South and the 'middle ground' of the frontier. In this guise, he assumed important roles in public office and was elected to Congress in 1890. But he never masked his disappointment with his party, or his criticism of its rapid degeneration into a party governed by patronage, oligarchy and plutocracy.

When the Democratic senator Joseph Brown blocked a measure to recognise the favourable tariffs that had been granted to parliamentarians on the Louisville line during the Southern Great Exposition in 1883, Watson unhesitatingly resigned in disgust from Georgia's Parliament. He had been elected to that body two years previously and had waged a hard-fought battle for the counties to tax the big rail owners. And, in 1892, he abandoned the Democratic Party amidst much hubbub, even before the foundation of the People's Party. He denounced the degeneration of the Democratic Party and its betrayal of its values:

Did [Jefferson] dream that in 100 years or less his party would be prostituted to the vilest purposes of monopoly;

---

11   Kazin, *The Populist Persuasion*, p. 10

that redeyed Jewish millionaires would be chiefs of that Party, and that the liberty and prosperity of the country would be ... constantly and corruptly sacrificed to Plutocratic greed in the name of Jeffersonian Democracy?

James Weaver shared a similar profile, as the Populist Party's frontman in the 1890s and its candidate for the 1892 presidential contest, in which he achieved a considerable success. The son of a family of Ohio pioneers who had moved to Iowa following the frontier, Weaver, too, was a lawyer and then a district attorney, a great public speaker and a skilled journalist. He first devoted his energies to Lincoln's Republican Party, also winning a seat in Congress, before then passing to the Greenback Party, an independent formation that fought for an anti-deflationary policy to the benefit of small farmers and a growing mass of industrial workers.

He fought for progressive taxation, against the repression of the trade unions, against the private monopolies in rail and communications, for the election of the Senate by direct suffrage, and then, from the late 1880s onward, for unlimited silver coinage. This programme was the child of what Mark Twain called the *Gilded Age*[12] in the final decades of the nineteenth century, when the United States experienced a new great transformation, with the rise of immense concentrations of industrial and financial power, the boom in the banks and railways, and the emergence of great mechanised industries based on the American system, i.e. mass assembly lines, and giant mining firms. At the same time, this age also saw the impoverishment of marginal and

---

12 Mark Twain (with Charles Dudley Warner), *The Gilded Age: A Tale of Today*, American Publishing Company, Hartford, CT, 1873.

rural areas, of the vast army of small agricultural proprietors who had driven forth the 'frontier', and of the urbanised masses in the nascent industrial cities. Here, notwithstanding the accelerated growth in the wages of high-skilled workers in particular, a war broke out among the poor, fuelled by the flows of migrants.[13]

Economic historians calculate that in the last decade of the nineteenth century the richest 1 per cent of the US population owned around 51 per cent of the entire nation's wealth, with only 1.1 per cent left for the bottom 44 per cent! This was the age of the 'robber barons', the new lords of an America that now benefited from unprecedented inequality: from the steel king Andrew Carnegie to the rail tycoons Jay Gould, Mark Hopkins and Collins Potter Huntington, the oil magnate John D. Rockefeller, J.P. Morgan in high finance and John W. Gates, the inventor and monopolist of barbed wire. They dominated from an ever loftier position a mass of ever more dependent workers faced with extremely harsh working conditions (a sixty-hour working week was then the norm) which were also very dangerous, with the highest percentage of accidents in the world (in 1889 there were over 20,000 injuries and almost 2,000 deaths among the 700,000 workers on the railways).[14] The money accumulated at the peak

---

13   Charles W. Calhoun (ed.), *The Gilded Age: Perspectives on the Origins of Modern America*, Rowman & Littlefield, Lanham, MD, 2007; Robert W. Cherny, *American Politics in the Gilded Age, 1868–1900*, Harlan Davidson, Wheeling, IL, 1997; Jack Beatty, *Age of Betrayal: The Triumph of Money in America, 1865–1900*, Vintage Books, New York, 2008.

14   George Brown Tindall and David E. Shi, *America: A Narrative History*, 9th ed., W. W. Norton & C., New York, 2012, vol. II, p. 590; Walter Licht, *Nineteenth-century American Railwaymen: A Study in the Nature and Organization of Work*, Princeton University Press, Princeton, NJ, 1977, pp. 190–1.

of the social pyramid was also rapidly co-opting the political sphere, buying off or in any case shaping the emerging political machines – the apparatuses of the great national parties, concentrated in the big cities. Given the combination of these prevailing conditions, it is almost inevitable that a programme of radical moral and political opposition began to develop (even if for an only brief period), emerging particularly strongly from the peripheral areas of society.

James Weaver's presidential candidacy in 1892 met with unexpected – and unhoped-for – success, especially in the states making up the US's heartlands in what their natives called the Great Plains, in the wide strip flanking the 100th meridian, from Texas in the South to Dakota in the North, with significant further encroachments to both the East and West.

The populist candidate won in five states: in Colorado with 57 per cent, in Kansas with 50.2 per cent, in North Dakota with 49 per cent, and in Idaho and Nevada with 54 per cent and 67 per cent respectively. He came in second place in South Dakota, Nebraska and Wyoming with scores around 40 per cent. And he also came second in Texas, albeit with a lower percentage of the vote. He also secured sporadic good results in contiguous areas along the eastern strip running from the Great Lakes down to Florida, adjacent to the mountain region that separates the Great Plains from the East Coast: from 36 per cent in Alabama to 19 per cent in Mississippi and Georgia, 14 per cent in Florida, 11 per cent in Minnesota and 9 per cent in Tennessee.

Weaver and his comrades in the People's Party thought – or deluded themselves – that this was just the beginning.[15] Yet theirs

---

15 'Unaided by money – Weaver commented at the time – our grand young party has made an enviable record and achieved a surprising success

was an ephemeral success. Already, the 1896 presidential election set them on the back foot, and with the sidelining of their original programme they also changed their 'values', at least in part. With the turn of the century, the values of the populists as a whole, including Weaver and especially Watson, shifted from the initial advocacy of unity among white and black workers to an incipient racism, or in any case a competitive view of 'separateness' that flirted with the segregationist impulses of the South. At the same time, they were attracted toward an explicit anti-Semitism that pointed to the Jew as emblematic of the power that money and the metropolitan oligarchies exercised over the producer-people.[16] And yet the 'electoral geography' revealed by the 1892 vote would prove far tougher and more resilient than its temporary spokesmen. It was destined to continue burrowing away, unseen, in the political subsoil of Deep America, with its charge of radicalism. And of ambiguity.

The apprentice – the shock

It may seem bizarre or even incredible, but the same electoral geography reappeared a century and a quarter later, at the end of 2016, in what has been considered the most transgressive and

---

at the polls' (cited Robert B. Mitchell, *Skirmisher: The Life, Times, and Political Career of James B. Weaver*, Edinburgh Press, Roseville, MN, 2008, p. 176). For this and other US electoral data cited in this volume, see *Dave Leip's Atlas of US Presidential Elections*, uselectionatlas.org.

16 Indicative – and disconcerting – was the position Thomas Watson took on the 'Frank case', in which a Georgian industrialist was accused of murdering a thirteen-year-old female worker and condemned to death. Described in Comer Vann Woodward, *Tom Watson: Agrarian Rebel*, Oxford University Press, Oxford, 1938, p. 386.

disconcerting of American presidential contests. This result was unforeseeable, and unforeseen.

The night of 8 November 2016 saw six hours that shook the world. It was as if we had prepared to look out over the calm surface of a lake, but instead saw the disturbing image of the Loch Ness monster emerging from the depths. And, in this, we also experienced the collapse of many of the myths of our time. The myth of the omnipotence of the establishment. The myth of the omniscience of the pollsters and well-briefed journalists. The myth of the media system's unchallenged capacity to condition the electorate. And it is difficult to forget the faces of the most popular anchormen from the main TV networks, around the world, turning to glass. They were bewildered, lost in the void, like the brokers on the world's stock markets on all history's worst 'Black Tuesdays'. The uncontrolled agitation of CNN's John King, standing in front of his magic touchscreen wall, when the colours of the states called for each candidate began to run out of control and he had to admit, disconsolate, that none of the news that the polls had been preparing us for had come true. Or the desperate comments of the CBS star Stephen Colbert, when at the end of a night of torture, with Donald Trump now uncatchable, he asked himself (and America): 'Were there crazier moments than what's happening right now? Or is this just the ultimate fruit of the crazy tree?' The journalist Mark Alperin beside him added, in apocalyptic terms, that 'Outside of the Civil War, World War II and including 9/11, this may be the most cataclysmic event the country's ever seen'.[17] As *The New York Times* commented, it was as if 'an

---

17   Dave Itzkoff, 'For Stephen Colbert, a Very Uncomfortable Election Night', *The New York Times*, 9 November 2016.

asteroid had hit' all of American television, one studio after another.[18]

In a world left open-mouthed – what the poet would call 'stricken and stunned'[19] – this was the dominant attitude among dailies across the West. It was as if the impossible had suddenly materialised. And as if we found ourselves living in an unknown reality. Britain's *Daily Mirror* ran a full-page front-cover image of the Statue of Liberty with its hands clasped over its face in horror. The tweet 'What Have They Done?'; 'Dear God, America what have you done?' was also quoted by *The Daily Telegraph*, while the image of the faces of the four presidents on Mount Rushmore with an expression of absolute despair spread virally on social media. France's *Libération* headlined 'Trumpocalypse' and *Le Figaro* went with 'The Hurricane', while François Hollande's ambassador in Washington, Gérard Araud – something of a star on the web – issued a far from diplomatic tweet: 'After Brexit and this election, everything is now possible. A world is collapsing before our eyes.' *The Daily Telegraph* limited itself to the more composed but no less stark headline 'Trump's American Revolution', while New York's *Daily News* ran a photo of the White House superimposed with 'House of Horrors!' in block capitals. A sign of how great the shock was, at least as much as the surprise.

But perhaps that such a result could have occurred should not have been so unexpected; our response so uncomprehending. What happened was not a flash of lightning in a clear blue sky. To understand this, we just needed to look beyond the surface level of

---

18   James Poniewozikr, 'A Rudderless Night, as News Networks Struggle With a Surprise Victory', *The New York Times*, 9 November 2016.

19   Percossa, attonita – in the words of Alessandro Manzoni's *Il cinque maggio*.

the United States itself. We should have avoided simply trusting – and relying on – the majority narrative in the central points of the nation's connective tissue, where an ever more condensed life runs at an ever faster pace. Rather, we needed to do more to put our ear to the ground and hear the rumbling of *l'Amérique profonde*. And, at the same time, to understand that a complex country like the United States does not have a single synchronised and uniform time. Rather, it moves at different speeds, and alongside the temporal vertigo of world trade and globalised society there are also other, enduring temporalities that point in an opposite direction. The speed at surface level can marginalise these other temporalities, but they survive nonetheless, and sporadically re-emerge in individual and collective behaviours. The red splash colouring in the territories conquered by Trump bears the mark of a *longue durée*, as well as the mark of new forms of suffering.

Maps (old and new)

On the night of 8 November 2016 various global networks offered internet users interactive maps, from which it was possible to see the geography of the vote take shape in real time, just like on John King's touchscreen wall on CNN. *The Guardian* in particular offered an extraordinarily interesting map in which it was possible not only to track the states being declared for one or another candidate, but also the count in the individual counties. A simple zoom function allowed us to take a closer look and, once the results were in, to observe the colourful spectacle at various different levels.

From the first indications, I could not fail to note the unbroken red strip – a uniform bright red – running vertically from South to North, from Texas to North Dakota. That is, the regions of the

Great Plains; the same areas which the People's Party painted in its own colours so many decades before – a whole aeon, we could say. In seven of the nine states where James Weaver came first or second, Trump scored huge victories (as the CNBC journalists commented on the night, 'the reddest of the red' counties were concentrated in these same regions).[20] Trump took Wyoming with 70 per cent of the vote, South and North Dakota with 61 per cent and 64 per cent respectively, Nebraska with 60 per cent, Idaho with 59 per cent and Kansas with 57 per cent. Of the states racked up by Weaver back in 1892, Trump missed out only in Nevada and Colorado. But, if we zoom in on this first state, for example, we see right away that it went to Clinton thanks to her success in just one of the sixteen counties, the most populous, Las Vegas,[21] while all the others went to Trump with huge margins. Hence, this territory which 'from above', at the statewide level, appears in a uniform blue, turns red when we look at it 'on the ground', at the county level. Colorado was little different, especially when we examine its eastern areas.

But this game of changing colours does not apply only to the individual states (or to limited cases). It can also be usefully applied to the entire national picture, looking at the interactive map as a whole. Then we can see the – itself rather disconcerting – spectacle of an equally rather blurred picture, with significant portions of blue wedged in here and there, which suddenly

---

20   Mark Fahey and Nicholas Wells, 'The reddest of the red, the bluest of the blue', CNBC, cnbc.com.

21   Las Vegas brought 401,068 Democratic votes, in the only blue patch, surrounded by an unbroken red carpet of far less populated locations (with between 3,000 and 20,000 voters) in which Trump won by enormous margins (from a maximum of 84 per cent to 8 per cent, to a minimum of 59 per cent to 31 per cent, with an average margin of around 60 per cent).

become redder as we look in closer detail and see all the individual patches 'occupied by Trump's troops'. The large central areas thus come to look a homogenous red, with only the eastern and western coastal strips uniformly coloured in blue. This owes to the – itself striking – fact that Trump racked up some 2,623 of the 3,142 counties in the contest (a historic record), while only 487 were left over for Clinton. The radical Right could thus use visual trickery to give credence to the false idea that Trump had achieved a general landslide in the popular vote, masking the reality that the 'Trump' areas were the least populated and the 'Hilary' ones the most densely populated;[22] indeed the final count showed that she had taken a total of 65,844,610 votes against his 62,979,636.

Two Americas

Be that as it may, once we have left aside the most transparent manipulation and self-interested conjecture, it remains true – and

---

22   The Breitbart News Network formerly directed by important Trump advisor Steve Bannon, which can be defined as a 'right-wing or far-right American website' (Wikipedia), particularly distinguished itself in this regard. On 15 November 2016 it published an aggressive article by Michael Patrick Leahy entitled 'Donald Trump Won 7.5 Million Popular Vote Landslide in Heartland', accompanied by a striking map almost wholly coloured in a homogeneous brick red and with only two thin blue strips on the extreme edges, i.e. the West and East coasts. Not a Democratic-aligned paper but the authoritative (and conservative) *Washington Post* attempted to deconstruct this evident optical illusion, with Philip Bump's article entitled 'Thanks to a bad map and bizarre math, Breitbart can report that Trump won the REAL popular vote', *The Washington Post*, 15 November 2016. Similar to Bump's line was that taken by Eren Moreno, 'Did you know? Trump Won 2,626 Counties. Hillary Only Won 487', Truthfeed.com, 6 December 2016.

this is itself a stunning development – that the November 2016 contest produced a compellingly different picture of the United States. And the image that clearly comes into relief is that of a country sharply divided in two. In some senses, a picture of two countries, or two nations, which are also territorially separate. *The New York Times*, also making use of the telling election maps, spoke of the 'Two Americas'.[23] There is 'Trump's America' – a territorially vast country, spanning 3 million square miles or 85 per cent of US territory (in which, however, only 146 million people, 46 per cent of the total US population, live). Then there is Clinton's America – an incredibly dense and concentrated country, very limited in spatial terms, covering 530,000 square miles, barely 15 per cent of US territory, but also very highly populated (174 million people, 54 per cent of the US population and almost 30 million more than Trump's America).

These two worlds are anthropologically, economically, socially and culturally foreign to one another. The chasm between them seems to reflect a cleavage widely identified by political scientists who describe the state-building (and in part also nation-building) process – i.e. the formation of modern nation states – but which seemed to have fallen into relative disuse in modern times. Namely, the cleavage that separates centre and periphery or city and countryside.[24] Trump's America is the rural America of scattered houses and farms lost amidst the prairies; the America of half-depopulated villages and small provincial centres ever more disconnected from their respective capitals; the America of the peripheries, of all the isolated peripheries forgotten by the centres.

---

23   Tim Wallace, 'The Two Americas of 2016', *The New York Times*, 16 November 2016.

24   See in particular the works of Stein Rokkan.

Clinton's America, conversely, is the metropolitan America of the big and especially the very biggest cities; or rather, of the metropoles' central districts. This is the America of the centre of the centres, where she won by enormous margins, for instance in DC (93 per cent to 4 per cent – an 89 per cent gap) or in the Bronx (89 per cent to 10 per cent), Manhattan (87 per cent to 10 per cent) or, on the opposite coast, San Francisco (85 per cent to 10) and Los Angeles (71 per cent to 23 per cent). The statistics tell us that, in the urban cores (sixty-eight counties in total, but with huge electoral weight), Clinton triumphed by an average 72-percentage-point margin. Conversely, Trump monopolised the rural vote (1,299 counties) with an average 86-percentage-point advantage, and in very small and small cities (637 and 356 counties) with 73- and 70-point margins respectively. He also took the medium-sized cities and the suburbs with margins of around 50 percentage points.[25]

Things were not always like this. The United States was not always so polarised, at least during the 'short twentieth century'. We need only look at the electoral map over time[26] to see that even as recently as the beginning of the 1990s the distribution of colours still appeared relatively mixed, with blue and red patches intermingling and large white spaces (where the two contenders tied) more or less everywhere. The other Clinton, Bill, was the last Democratic candidate to achieve a draw in the total count of

---

25 Lazaro Gamio and Dan Keat, 'How Trump redrew the electoral map, from sea to shining sea', *The Washington Post*, 9 November 2016.

26 See the series of maps appearing in *The New York Times* alongside Gregor Aisch, Adam Pearce and Karen Yourish's article, 'The Divide Between Red and Blue America Grew Even Deeper in 2016', 10 November 2016.

counties, when he won around 1,500 counties in 1992, more or less as many as Bush Sr. In 2000, Al Gore fell below 700, and in 2012, Barack Obama took fewer than 600 (even if he won eighty-six of the most populated hundred). The 'Heartlands' and in particular the central strip represented by the Great Plains were no impregnable Republican stronghold: in 1964 Lyndon Johnson had romped home in these regions, as had Franklin D. Roosevelt in 1932. Only in the final decade of the twentieth century did the two Americas establish themselves in their respective territories and begin to grow apart, first gradually and then ever more rapidly.

At first this was a sort of underground faultline which, only in its final phase, became an earthquake (*in fine velocior*, as the Romans put it); Trump's victory was but the eventual result of a process of medium- or longer-term duration. We see this in the electoral statistics, which do not just provide a static photograph of the result but register its dynamics. For instance, the statistics which count and compare the landslide counties, i.e., those where one of the candidates won by at least 20 percentage points. As recently as 1992, these were shared out in balanced proportions (553 for the Democrats, 592 for the Republicans) and counted for less than a third of the total. By 2016, the number of Democratic landslide counties had more than halved, as they fell to 242, while the Republican figure quadrupled, soaring to 2,232 (and landslide counties amounted to over five-sixths of Trump's total!)

This is a symptom of the entrenchment and radicalisation of the electorate on each side, with a growth in Republican support (at least in terms of geographical extension) particularly linked to the figure of Donald Trump. Studying the data, we see that he had a particular capacity to 'shift' votes (another key aspect of the political dynamic). He deepened his roots in districts that were already 'his' (traditionally Republican ones) and above all stripped new areas from his opponent, confirming the arguments of those who underline the particular 'energy' of political populism.[27] And this also confirms populism's ability to 'mobilise' normally passive layers of the electorate or to shift the sentiments of active ones. Trump won more votes than 2012 Republican nominee Mitt Romney had in the last presidential contest in 2,728 counties, while Clinton beat Obama's result in 383. Trump took 220 counties from his opponent (ones that Obama had won in 2012), while Clinton prevailed in only seventeen counties that Romney had won. This was, substantially, key to his victory and her defeat.

After the fact – 'when the funeral's over' – all the political analysts and commentators say the same thing: Trump won thanks to his unexpected capacity to win almost all the so-called swing states, some of which were traditionally Democratic strongholds. And he did this as the 'perfect populist', overwhelming all the traditional political cultures and moving transversally outside and against the various party apparatuses – his opponent's but also, indeed first of all, his own! He did it by playing on the articulated 'moral economies' of an electorate characterised by various different moods of loss or deprivation, united by the feeling that they had been pushed back into a 'marginal' position, whether in terms of their status, role, self-image or income.

This leads us to a particularly hot topic of the American election and its populist backdrop – a delicate and indeed controversial theme – namely the impact of the working class (or better, 'white working class') and its supposed or real realignment. After all, the 'swing states' are largely the states of the so-called Rust

---

27   Kazin, *The Populist Persuasion*, p. 12.

Belt, located in the once prosperous traditional industrial areas (the old Steel Belt) which are now partly abandoned. Other swing states are spread along the Appalachians, the 'highlands' with a considerable presence of coal and iron mines. These were home to the 'bastions' of Democratic strength built up in the industrial age, which had endured until 2012 and now fell to Trump. This was powerfully illustrated in a richly hued piece in *The New York Times*, which described the population of Pennsylvania's Wyoming River Valley, which having voted for Obama by double digits now turned en masse to Trump; and so, too, the string of old industrial towns spread along the edge of Lake Erie, who chose Obama last time, but now opted for Trump over Clinton by a 20-point margin.[28] A sizeable chunk, that is, of the famous 'basket of deplorables' – the term Hillary Clinton used to describe a good half of Trump's electorate[29] – giving form to the Gothic story of a party that suddenly sees its own most trusted social base transform, in a Kafkaesque metamorphosis, from a butterfly into a worm, to the point that it becomes tragically unrecognisable.

And, here, the focus of the analysis shifts from the territorial level to another cleavage of central importance for the political

---

28   Nate Cohn, 'Why Trump Won: Working-Class Whites', *The New York Times*, 9 November 2016.

29   The Democratic candidate used this unfortunate expression during a New York fundraiser organised by the LGBT community on 10 September 2016. Faced with vehement protests by the Trump campaign spokeswoman, who accused her of having insulted 'millions of Americans', and the reaction from Trump himself – attacking an insult against 'millions of amazing, hardworking people' – Clinton admitted her error of over-simplification, and made clear that she had meant to refer to the xenophobic, racist and sexist minority among Trump's supporters and not 'frustrated and angry' poor Americans.

scientist, typical of modernity: the social cleavage. This is the 'capital/labour' pairing, typically used to draw the once sharp boundary between Left and Right, and which now offers evidence of unprecedented shifts taking place.

The metamorphosis of the 'working class'

'Today the American working class is going to strike back, finally!' It may seem impossible to imagine such a line coming from one of the wealthiest men in the United States. But these were the words with which Donald Trump began his final campaign rally in Michigan. In this short speech he invited his listeners to 'dream big' and ran through the simple points that made up his programme (the border wall with Mexico, the cancellation of the North American Free Trade Agreement (NAFTA) and Trans-Pacific Partnership (TPP) free-trade deals, deporting Syrian refugees, and, most importantly, heavy taxes on companies outsourcing jobs, a return to traditional energy sources, as well as a merciless war against the corrupt media and politicians – 'the world's most dishonest people'). He promised that 'The forgotten men and women of our country will be forgotten no longer.' Hand on heart, he assured his listeners in his own style: 'I'm with you. I'll fight with you. I will win for you. I promise.' He said this to a crowd of ordinary people, many still dressed in their work clothes. Clinton, conversely, ended her campaign with Michelle and Barack Obama, Bill Clinton and Bruce Springsteen, in Philadelphia and then in Raleigh, North Carolina. In the elegant surroundings of the University's Reynolds Coliseum, Clinton spoke after Lady Gaga had performed her *I Want Your Love* and then sung *Livin' On A Prayer* in a duet with Bon Jovi.

All the most important media, who before the count had seen the contrast between these final rallies as proof of Trump's pathetic isolation, discovered with the benefit of hindsight the proof of his 'tactical genius'. The proof of his ability to see 'that there are really two Americas – and one has fatally neglected the other'.[30] Of the fact that there was a silent 'army of the discouraged' waiting for Trump to come along and mobilise them.[31] And the media now headed out like detectives on the traces of the 'working-class vote'. One such reporter was the *Telegraph* correspondent David Millward, who climbed aboard the Acela Express on 9 November, on what he calls a train for the prosperous. Indeed, it is a very expensive service, at $310 for a journey of under three hours, with all the mod-cons (free WiFi, lunch served at your seat, conference tables . . .). It links New York to Washington, passing via the Northeast Corridor, Trenton, Philadelphia, Baltimore, tacking along the borders between New Jersey and Pennsylvania and then between Maryland and Delaware, the backbone of an old American industrial heartland. The Acela's passengers – businessmen, lobbyists travelling to the capital, politicians of various levels, the jet set – for the most part remain hunched over their laptops or immersed in the music coming from their headphones. But if they did glance at the landscape outside the windows, as Millward does, they would see a continual stream of empty warehouses, abandoned factories, broken windows, weeds growing in the squares, and the walls of

---

30   David Millward, 'Donald Trump saw that there are really two Americas – and one has fatally neglected the other', *The Telegraph*, 10 November 2016.
31   David Lightman, 'The age of Trump begins, fuelled by social media', *The Seattle Times*, 9 November 2016.

what were once 'hives of activity' that offered 'millions of stable jobs' and have now turned into 'blank canvases' for writers' fantasies. They are the compelling image of a de-industrialised America. And the Acela Express, with its contrast between 'inside' and 'outside', is the physical metaphor for the two Americas that clashed in the November 2016 vote. As the write-up of Millward's journey suggests, the motto of Trump's campaign – 'Make America Great Again' – touched a nerve with the 'outsiders', the 'millions of disenchanted blue-collar' Americans, whereas Clinton got the backing of those 'inside', or 'on top' – the Americans in business class.[32]

The two reporters from the Associated Press found this same scenario[33] not much further to the west, in Elliott County, renowned for having voted Democratic without interruption for almost 150 years and now turning en masse in favour of Trump, who humiliated Clinton here by a clear 70 to 25 per cent margin. Still ringing in the ears of the residents of this 'coal-infused' county, in the heart of Kentucky's mining country, were the words pronounced right here, a few months before, by the candidate of what ought to have been their party, when she told an audience of environmentalists that she wanted to put the coal mines and coal miners 'out of business'. These voters were also infuriated by Obama's 'green economy'. Here, this meant poverty, in an area that has not seen the economic recovery, where the unemployment rate is above 11 per cent (more than double the national average of 4.6 per cent) and where the average family income hovers around $28,000, a hair's breadth above half the US average.

---

32 Millward, 'Donald Trump saw that there are really two Americas'.
33 Laurie Kellman and Adam Beam, 'Trump Country. What one county tells us about the election', Associated Press, 13 November 2016.

Such were the narratives that came after the fact. But we need only have paid the slightest attention to a book published a few months beforehand, commenting on Trump's stunning success in the Republican primaries, to hear the threatening rumbles coming from Deep America and understand that the contest was far from over. It was entitled *The Gilded Rage: A Wild Ride through Donald Trump's America* [34] and it explored the 'popular bitterness' and the 'fury' he was able to direct against élites, as it drew up an unexpected identikit image of 'Trump's army'. Or rather, of its 'hard core', which allowed him to tear like a cyclone through the Republican establishment, overcoming the 'thoroughbreds' one by one in the primaries and then winning the final duel with Clinton for the White House. These were 'the discarded veterans of the endless wars in the Middle East, the blue-collar workers who will never again match the money they made when they were young, the residents of rural hamlets and suburban outposts that are always overlooked by the media radar'.[35] That is, the people inhabiting the 'underside of the American Dream', whom 'the Donald' offered an unexpected opportunity to scale the castle walls and 'hang the last Clinton with the guts of the last Bush'.[36]

Seventy-five per cent of Trump's voters – we are told by the author, an independent journalist with a taste for exploring matters at ground level – are made up of people who 'say their lives have steadily gotten worse over the last five decades.' He describes how he met them in the bars or parking lots next to the

---

34 Alexander Zaitchik, *The Gilded Rage: A Wild Ride through Donald Trump's America*, Hot Books, New York, 2016.
35 David Talbot, 'Foreword', ibid., p. iii.
36 Ibid., p. 3.

electoral rallies (sporting obscene T-shirts with slogans like 'Hillary Sucks, but not like Monica' and 'Trump That Bitch') and sometimes in their houses, shacks or trailers. Such was his 'wild ride' through 'Trumpland', from Arizona to California, centring on the triangle made up of Wisconsin, Pennsylvania and West Virginia, the states which saw the great swing that made the difference in the election. These were, in large measure, the states of the 'humiliated working class'.

One such case is Clairton, the town of 8,000 inhabitants in the heart of Pennsylvania where the first part of Michael Cimino's film *The Deer Hunter* is set. This community sprung up in the surroundings of the US Steel coal ovens, but already in 1978, when *The Deer Hunter* was being shot, deep cracks were already becoming visible behind a still respectable façade. It now 'resembled the abandoned industrial town at the beginning of Tarkovsky's *Stalker*. The main drag is a museum of shuttered businesses under faded signs from another age'. Around this main drag, we see old miners afflicted by silicosis or cancer – professional diseases for whoever digs coal – some of them with an oxygen canister strapped to their trolleys; and so, too, young men left underemployed since the union was pushed out of the surviving mines. Now there is work only four days a week, without limits on working hours and with pay levels below those of the 1980s. These are people who had stopped believing in anyone, but who now opted for Trump as their 'last hope'. 'In the beginning', one local observes, 'I thought, "Trump, this guy is an asshole". He's arrogant and crass, I'll give you that . . . But I believe the way that he thinks can do what has to be done.'[37] In Fayette and Green counties, the coal-mining heart of

---

37 Ibid.

working-class Pennsylvania, where in his day Bill Clinton thrashed Bob Dole by 30 points, today Trump beat Clinton by 65 per cent to 33 per cent and 69 per cent to 28 per cent, respectively!

Matters are no different in West Virginia, the barycentre of the crisis of the United States' old economy: 'poor, poorly educated, overwhelmingly white, in economic free fall . . . A state that, like Trump, seemed a caricature of itself, a toothless monster of working-class anger, despair, alienation, bitterness, and defiance.'[38] West Virginia was always a rebellious region. In 1921, the minors of Mingo County, on the mountainous border with Pennsylvania, fought the battle of Blair Mountain,[39] 'one of American labor's greatest and bloodiest rebellions'. Ten thousand armed strikers, fighting for union recognition, battled with 3,000 scabs and gunslingers hired by the sheriff. Today, in Mingo (where in 1996 Bill beat Dole 70 per cent to 20 per cent), Trump defeated Clinton by 83 per cent to 14 per cent.

And the same thing has happened in Whitesville, another site of key symbolic importance in the epic history of coal, because it was there that one of the worst mining tragedies in modern America, the 'Upper Big Branch Mine Disaster', took place in 2010. Twenty-nine miners were killed after an underground explosion. The town also counts large numbers of victims of coal dust, including dozens upon dozens of children.

The population of Whitesville is 99.23 per cent white, the mean income is $13,274 per head and 30 per cent of the inhabitants live below the poverty line. Trump won with 75 per cent of the vote,

---

38   Ibid., p. 51.
39   Robert Shogan, *The Battle of Blair Mountain: The Story of America's Largest Union Uprising*, Westview Press, Boulder, CO, 2004.

also thanks to his open display of being 'politically incorrect "about trade, the vets, Social Security, Mexicans, Muslims, busty broads – about so many things" '.[40] A comforting sound for those who have been pushed utterly to the margins. This was equally well explained by another short flurry of books, close to ignored at their moment of publication but precious guides after the disaster of 8 November 2016. These books had explicit titles, with recurrent terms like *Angry White Man*[41], *White Rage* (anger right on the front cover, again!)[42] or *White Trash*[43]. Added to these is perhaps the richest text on the metamorphosis and rancorous alienation built up on the 'underside of the American Dream'. What we could define an identikit within the identikit of the American syndrome.

Hillbilly Elegy

The hillbilly is a human type. In many regards, a stereotype. He is the flesh-and-blood embodiment of an anthropological profile.

In the strict sense – in topographical terms – those who truly belong to this category are the 'highlanders' or 'Appalachians'

---

40   Zaitchik, *The Gilded Rage*, Introduction, p. 73.

41   Michael Kimmel, *Angry White Man: Masculinity at the End of an Era*, Nation Books, New York, 2013, on the 'gender' frustrations of the American male faced with the crisis of his sexual but also social and political roles.

42   Carol Anderson, *White Rage: The Unspoken Truth of our Racial Divide*, Bloomsbury, New York, 2016, on the crisis of multiracialism in the US city peripheries.

43   Nancy Isenberg, *White Trash: The 400-Year Untold History of Class in America*, Viking, New York, 2016, on the multiple intersections between class and race in today's existential disorder.

scattered across the long strip of hills and mountains running from Alabama and Georgia to the North, up to the Canadian border, straddling North Carolina and Pennsylvania on one side and Tennessee, Kentucky and West Virginia on the other. But their most important associations are ethnic (the original core are Scots-Irish, from the first wave of immigration) and cultural; or rather, sociocultural. As the *New York Journal* put it in 1900, more or less when this term began to be used:

> a Hill-Billie is a free and untrammeled white citizen of Tennessee, who lives in the hills, has no means to speak of, dresses as he can, talks as he pleases, drinks whiskey when he gets it, and fires off his revolver as the fancy takes him.

Added to all this, the hillbilly is poor. His is a rustic, dignified poverty (or so it was for a long time – today much less so), rooted in history and in the isolation that has existed ever since the frontier, which long stood here, proceeded further West. This left these harsh and rather wild lands to play a service (or subordinate) role for the powerful industrial poles of the East Coast and the Great Lakes: the dirty jobs of digging coal and iron for the assembly lines of Detroit and Chicago.[44]

One of the hillbillies' more fortunate sons, J.D. Vance, dedicated a profound, prophetic book to them, with the poetic title *Hillbilly Elegy*.[45] One of the few who managed to extricate himself from this condition, Vance received his degree from Yale Law School and

---

44 Anthony Harkins, *Hillbilly. A Cultural History of an American Icon*, Oxford University Press, Oxford, 2005.

45 J.D. Vance, *Hillbilly Elegy. A Memoir of a Family and Culture in Crisis*, HarperCollins, New York, 2016.

then moved to San Francisco (the hated metropolis), where he lives with his wife and two dogs. But as he himself writes, he is still pursued by the 'the demons of the life we left behind'.[46] This is why he tells us the story of a substance-abusing mother who brought many different men through the house. Of an absent father. Of a grandfather, Papaw, a cantankerous man never off the booze. A grandmother, Mamaw, abstemious and violent, who threatened to kill Vance's grandfather if he kept on drinking, and one time even trying to do it. But through an ancestral sense of family responsibility, the pair become the guardians of the young J.D., indeed allowing him – thanks to their support – to climb the academic ladder. A family just like so many others around here, scattered across the wooden hovels on the slopes of the hills standing over the Kentucky Highway 15, the ramshackle trailers, the low-cost, government-subsidised housing, and the small farms just like the one that serves as the 'backdrop for the author's "childhood memories" '. And, like these families, ' "From low social mobility to poverty to divorce and drug addiction", my home is a hub of misery.'[47]

All of them – mother and father, grandmother and grandfather, neighbours and classmates – are typical hillbillies, those who others pejoratively call rednecks or white trash but who they instead call 'neighbours, friends, brothers'.[48] Their forefathers were 'day laborers in the Southern slave economy, sharecroppers after that, coal miners after that, and machinists and millworkers during more recent times',[49] and now underemployed or precarious workers dependent on meagre government subsidies. Their

---

46 Ibid., p. 2.
47 Ibid., p. 4.
48 Ibid., p. 2.
49 Ibid., p. 3.

family story is nestled between Jackson, the small town (with 2,000 inhabitants) in the heart of coal-mining Kentucky where Vance was born, and Middletown, Ohio, the company town that emerged in the surroundings of Armco Steel, where Papaw moved with Mamaw to work in the factory.

In Jackson (named after president Andrew Jackson), in 2016 Trump romped home with 89 per cent of the vote, and in the county of which this town is the main centre he took three-quarters of the vote, while Clinton could do no better than 27 per cent, much as in all the mining districts of this 'dark and bloody ground'. The historic United Mine Workers of America (UMWA) union was born there amidst bitter and hard-fought clashes, but the same people who used to wear baseball caps bearing the words 'God, Guns and Guts made the UMWA' now wear identical red hats with the Trump campaign slogan 'Make America Great Again'. More or less the same thing happened in Middletown. In Warren and Butler counties, whose boundaries the city straddles, where Trump won by 66 and 62 per cent respectively (a total of 184,619 votes, almost exactly double Clinton's tally of 92,372).

Papaw cast his first and only vote for a Republican – Ronald Reagan. Winning large blocks of Rust Belt Democrats like Papaw, Reagan went on to the biggest electoral landslide in modern American history. The hillbillies who had become blue-collar workers, he makes clear, had no love for Reagan. But they had even more hatred for 'that son of a bitch Mondale . . . a well-educated Northern liberal'.[50] Here was an open cultural clash: the people of the Great Appalachians had no trust in well-heeled types coming from the outside and, in general, whoever was 'different from us, whether the difference lies in how they look, how they

---

50   Ibid., p. 47.

act, or, most important, important, how they talk'.[51] Now Trump has repeated Reagan's performance with almost the same percentages, albeit in a town that has today totally changed. Today he is capturing not the pride of these mountain-based workers, proud of their independence, but rather their funeral song.

At the beginning of the 1980s, Middletown was a crown jewel in what was then the 'Steel Belt', before it began to 'rust'. It was a company town that rose up around the biggest coal-fed steel plant in the United States, established at the beginning of the twentieth century. There stood the company headquarters and its gigantic steel mill; the whole area's social life – sport, culture, social services, company welfare, citizens' home lives and leisure time – revolved around them.[52] So it remained until everything changed, and 'the company' became separate from the town. Japan's Kawasaki Steel Corporation took over ownership, the name changed to AK Steel, the headquarters migrated elsewhere, the factory was emptied out and cut back to minimum operations. So, too, did auxiliary jobs dry up, and the town became one of the many deindustrialised areas of the Rust Belt. It is one of the highest-ranked towns in the table of the US's most polluted areas.[53]

---

51 Ibid., p. 3.

52 For this reason, as part of his compassionate conservatism, Reagan himself used the town as an example of a community independent of government and public spending: see Nathaniel Sheppard, 'Middletown Ohio. A model for "Private Initiative" ', *The New York Times*, 15 December 1981.

53 Vance writes of 40 per cent childhood poverty in the suburbs. He cites a Brookings Institution study according to which the vast majority of residents in the surrounding area in conditions of extreme poverty – a situation that spread above all between 2005 and 2009 – were 'white, native-born, high school or college graduates, homeowners, and not receiving public assistance': Vance, *Hillbilly Elegy*, p. 51.

But it is not just Jackson and Middletown. The large majority of hillbillies rallied behind Trump, from the northern counties of Georgia and Alabama way up to the western counties of Pennsylvania and Ohio. He raked in votes in these areas, with leads ranging between 40 and 70 per cent. This owed not only to the 'social' messaging in his programme, his promise of a return to a proud past and a crude sense of greatness. It also owed to a sort of 'ethological' reflex in the mechanism of recognition, in the identification with elemental signs, gestures, expressions, smells and colours. They somehow saw Trump as 'someone like them', despite the vast divides of income and wealth that separated them – the fact that they stand at opposite ends of the social pyramid. They saw him as someone who 'looked' like them, with his wrestler's swagger, his kitsch style, the keenly paraded brutishness of his approach; someone who 'acted' like them, with an abruptness that looked like frankness, a muscular style, a disdain for formal rules and political correctness, a bull in a china shop act. Above all, they saw him as someone who 'spoke' like them, with his vulgarity, his dialogue-as-duel, using speech like a loaded handgun. They saw their own reflection in the image that the mainstream media, the big papers and the national TV networks offered of him, in disgusted tones; he, too, was 'white trash', a sort of 'redneck', not welcome at any dinner party. In short, an underdog, just like they themselves felt they were viewed and considered by the establishment of all sides and all colours. And they turned resoundingly in his favour.

'Underdogs' and 'fat cats'

'Underdogs rise up and bite fat cats.' Such was the front-page headline of Australia's hard-right *Daily Telegraph Sydney* on the morning of 10 November 2016. The article, written by Miranda Devine, was a sort of war despatch: 'Nobody wanted Trump to win except the voters.' 'It's the revenge of the deplorables. The silent majority has roared . . . The outsiders have given a black eye to the Establishment, just as they did with Brexit in the UK.'

Such was the birth certificate for a 'new breed of right-wing populism', with a geographical expanse just as transnational as the neoliberal paradigm that grew in tandem with globalisation. The sign of the shattering of the West's cultural-political matrix and an earthquake in its social composition. For, if the Right is discovering the 'working class', that means that something is broken. Deeply broken. First of all, within the working class. But also within the Right. And, above all, within the Left. It means that the Left has abandoned the field. Or better, that what was, historically, its social base – the 'subject' that made sense of its existence and provided a point of reference to its programmes – has migrated over to the other side. Which brings us into a now completely post-twentieth-century scenario.

Long debates have attempted to identify Trump's 'secret' and find the key to the 'miracle' that allowed his ascent. What 'spell' allowed him to pull the most stubborn conservatives behind him in a genuine revolution, and at the same time – precisely under the banner of conservation – pull along once-progressive Americans that now felt the blade of progress on their own skin? These debates sought some focal point to concentrate on; a common denominator for the bizarre 'social coalition' behind Trump.

Some said it was skin colour, saying that this was a white vote; or a gender one, saying that his voters were men with status anxiety whose standing in his family is in crisis. Others said it was a matter of education, emphasising the low qualification levels of most of his supporters.[54] These are all factors to which we will return, with proper attention, later on. But income is the factor on which most discussion has been concentrated; indeed, no few analysts have emphasised the role that the poor played in Trump's coalition. Or rather, they have argued that Trump's voters were 'the poor'. A closer reading of his electorate's income brackets nonetheless shows that he enjoyed greater support among those layers whose family incomes were above $50,000, and a particularly strong advantage among those between $100,000 and $200,000, while Clinton had the biggest lead – around a 12-percent advantage – among the under $30,000 bracket.[55] If the poor did indeed play a role – and in particular the poor left behind by mass-scale deindustrialisation – it was that their votes made up the 'marginal utility' of Trump's bid for the White House. They were the unexpected segment of the electorate which attached itself to the traditional, if now radicalised conservative base. And their extra weight was enough to tip the balance in the swing states.

So, despite the prevailing wisdom, the vote for Trump was not the revolt of the poor. It was, rather, the revenge of those who had been divested of something. All of them, even among the

---

54　Trump won 51 per cent to 45 per cent among those whose education level is 'High school or less', and 52 per cent to 43 per cent among those who have 'some college education' whereas Clinton won among 'college graduates' (49 per cent to 45 per cent) and postgraduates (scoring 58 per cent), though Trump nonetheless took 37 per cent of these latter.

55　Clinton won among those earning under $30,000 a year (53 per cent to 41 per cent) and between $30,000 and $49,999 (52 per cent to 42 per cent). Meanwhile Trump had a clear win among those earning between $50,000 and $99,999 (50 per cent to 46 per cent) and the contest was close to a tie among families with yet-higher incomes (around a one-point difference).

middle and upper classes, feel that they have somehow lost out: whether this means losing their male privilege, part of their income (however high), their social status, recognition of their work, respect for their faith or their country, their place in the world, their power, their hegemony . . . And they feel not only that they have lost these things, but that they have been divested of them by others: by finance, the banks, the 'swamp' of Washington, gays and lesbians and transgender people, Hollywood celebrities with no morals, the Hispanics who eat in their gardens, the Blacks who drop empty bottles in the streets, Muslims who have more faith than they do, the Arab oil magnates who buy up their cities and finance the throat-cutters . . . A multi-coloured army of traitors to the hardworking, god-fearing American people, distributed across the entire social scale.

Two more cleavages: race and gender

If we are to more accurately identify the characteristics of 'post-twentieth-century populism', it is worth setting two specific variables of the Trump vote within this wider context, namely racism and sexism. Or, we could say, the vote for Trump was character-ised by two other significant cleavages, of race and gender, on which the Republican candidate laid heavy emphasis throughout the presidential campaign. Indeed, it is obvious – as political analysts have keenly noted – that Trump drummed up a level of support among white voters that was in some regards unprece-dented in US electoral history (at least if we focus on 'knife's edge' presidential races where there was a small difference between the candidates, as in the case of the November 2016 contest). Trump won 58 per cent of white votes against just 37 per cent for Clinton (a 21-percentage-point difference). Not even in

2008, when a black candidate participated in the contest for the first time, did white voters rally together to this degree (back then, they had divided 55–43 per cent in favour of McCain, who thus had a 12-point advantage over Obama among whites).[56] In 1992 the white vote had split 39–40 per cent between Clinton and Bush; in 1996 this gap rose to just 3 points (43–46 per cent) in the Clinton–Dole contest. In 2008 Obama won the overall popular vote by a clear 53–46 per cent margin; as has been noted, this was 'because of his particular appeal among black voters, because of the changing political allegiances of Hispanics, *and because he did not provoke a backlash among white voters*'.[57] Eight years later, Hillary Clinton did not manage to do the same, even though in this case the 'salience' of race ought to have been nullified given that both contenders were white. Evidently, Donald Trump's strong rhetoric against ethnic minorities and his call for voters to express a sort of resurgent 'white pride' were, indeed, powerfully salient.

This is even more clear when we draw distinctions within the white electorate on the basis of education levels: the divide between 'college-educated whites' and 'non-college-educated whites'. While, among this former group, the gap between the two candidates was relatively limited (49 per cent for Trump versus 45 per cent for Clinton, in line with all the previous elections in which the white electorate on average preferred the Republicans) the

---

56 More than compensated by Obama's sweeping victory among Black voters (95 per cent, as against 4 per cent for McCain) and excellent result among Hispanics (67 per cent to 31 per cent).

57 Stephen Ansolabehere and Charles Stewart III, *Amazing Race*, *Boston Review*, January/February 2009, quoted in Brian F. Schaffner, 'Racial Salience and the Obama Vote', *Political Psychology* 32(6), December 2011.

difference soared among the non-college educated, among whom Trump (67 per cent) had a near 40-point gap over Clinton (28 per cent)! In a recent book on the 2016 presidential election, Brian F. Schaffner[58] analysed the medium-term shifts in the white vote according to education level (from 1980 to 2016). He reaches the interesting conclusion that in a first period from 1980 to 1996 'there was very little difference in how whites voted based on whether they had a college degree.'[59] But, after 1996, we see that 'the lines began to separate, with non-college-educated whites becoming more Republican in their vote choices', even if to a still relatively moderate degree: 'Thus, when Obama won in 2008, college-educated whites were far more supportive of him than non-college-educated whites, but both groups voted more Democratic than they had in the previous election.'[60] Only after then did the gap yawn far wider, as the less educated electorate radicalised along ethnic lines. In 2016, they would rally behind the candidate who knew better than any other how to pull the strings of their racial pride, and indeed deliberately sought to do so ('the 2016 election broke this pattern', Schaffner writes).[61] It is all too easy to see how the economic crisis that began precisely in 2008, having then produced all its destabilising effects, from 2012 onward played an important part in accelerating a tendency that was already underway under the surface. This factor must have lit the touchpaper (as has already been said) of the sense of *déclassement*, marginalisation and impoverishment among that part of the

---

58 Brian F. Schaffner, *Making Sense of the 2016 Elections: A CQ Press Guide*, SAGE Publications, Thousand Oaks, CA.

59 Ibid., p. 24.

60 Ibid., p. 25.

61 Ibid.

country that had traditionally been considered 'central' (the lower-middle classes and the white working class), which now discovered itself to be an insecure 'white minority' (in some cases, 'white trash') and, thus deprived of its position, sought a sort of social and political compensation.

This politically incorrect vote gave voice to what Carol Anderson calls 'white rage', the trigger for which, 'inevitably, is black advancement . . ., the blackness with ambition, with drive, with purpose, with aspiration, and with demands for full and equal citizenship'.[62] The support for the 'unfit' candidate Trump was the coarse yell of those who saw themselves slipping down the scale of the globalised economy, while others, who had until recently remained marginal and subaltern, seemed to be climbing it, or holding on, or in any case to be present in the thinking and attention of the political élites (no matter how hypocritical this apparent concern).

Those who mobilised for Trump were, in large part, the winners of the previous era in which America was great, who now discovered that they were the losers of globalisation, and for this reason sided with the least politically correct of politicians. Or rather, with the most politically incorrect, not only on questions of race (the politician most hostile to the minorities that these white voters, whose pride has been wounded, consider usurpers) but also the delicate question of gender. Indeed, it is telling that Trump catalysed the male vote – the vote of white men, above all married ones – to such a high degree. This election was marked by a sharp gender polarisation: Trump secured 53 per cent support among men as against 37 per cent among

---

62   Carol Anderson, *White Rage: The Unspoken Truth of Our Racial Divide*, Bloomsbury, New York, 2016, pp. 2–3.

women; conversely, Clinton obtained 41 per cent of the male vote as against 54 per cent of the female vote.

Here, too – it is worth emphasising – Trump clearly gave voice to the sense of frustration and fear felt by the traditional American male nostalgic for his old gender privileges and alarmed by the seemingly unstoppable rise of 'women's power', as detected in the changes in the prevalent mentality and language in the media-political sphere. And Trump did this by bringing into play his own personality, his own record as a womaniser dismissive of and disliked by women. He offered himself not only as a 'great communicator' but also as a 'great avenger' on the explosive terrain of bodily differences. It may seem paradoxical – though in fact, it is perfectly logical – that this largely rhetorical operation, above all conducted at the linguistic level with the use of an extreme, untamed, radically politically incorrect language, should have secured its best results in the 'peripheral' areas. That is, in those areas where, unlike the metropolitan centres, the concentration of the black and Latino population is lower (in some cases, it is outright non-existent) and the new frontiers of gender demands and mores are particularly weak, as traditional values have a greater effect on gender relations. It is only natural that this is how things should be: indeed, this is a mechanism that above all operates at the level of the imaginary. For it bases its judgement of current events less on concrete phenomena than on forms of representation (indeed, the representations produced by the mass media, by Hollywood, by the creators of the high-speed, postmodern narrative). And it was precisely on the terrain of narrative that there developed an identification between the deplorable Trump and his deplorable electorate.

A final question

What remains to be understood, however, is how those who were thus 'deprived' chose such a 'privileged' figure as their champion. Someone solidly established at the peak of the social pyramid. Not an outsider. Not a 'people's champion', or an average guy dedicated to the popular cause, but a tycoon. And at that, a tycoon from New York (which many of these voters do not even see as part of the same country!). This is what makes the populism of the twenty-first century different from any other that went before. Many journalists and even some scholars have sought to compare the forty-fifth president of the United States with the seventh – which is to say, the first 'populist' president, Andrew Jackson. They remind us that 'Washington insiders' considered Jackson 'intemperate, vulgar and stupid', calling him an 'ass' (hence the symbol of the Democratic Party, represented by a donkey).[63] And that, in private, Thomas Jefferson – the third US president – who knew Jackson well, termed him 'one of the most unfit men I know of' to become president of the United States, 'a dangerous man' who could not speak in a civilized manner because he would 'choke with rage'; a man whose 'passions are terrible'.[64] And if we are struck by Trump's wrestler-like strutting, his abrupt manner of speaking, his cult – and practice – of toughness (and 'tough' is the term that recurs most frequently in his self-description), Jackson, for his part, took part in no less than fourteen pistol duels with various rivals of his, and his final words on his deathbed concerned his only regret: that 'I did not

---

63 Dan P. McAdams, 'The Mind of Donald Trump', *The Atlantic*, June 2016.

64 Ibid.

shoot Henry Clay and I didn't hang John C. Calhoun' (his two toughest political opponents).

But Jackson really was 'a wild-haired mountain man',[65] an authentic hillbilly of pure Scots-Irish extraction, born somewhere in the Appalachians[66] between North and South Carolina to pioneers who had just migrated and were certainly not rich. Also for this reason, he was the figure best-suited to 'channel[ling] the crude sensibilities of the masses'.[67] Trump, conversely, was born into a wealthy family of powerful New York real estate tycoons. The fact that the rage of the deprived could identify with a billionaire – his wealth built on rent – is in a sense the watershed between the original populism and the populism that follows the end of the twentieth century. Such is the oxymoronic clash between 'on top' and 'down below' that has risen from the ashes of the twentieth-century Left/Right pairing.

---

65   Ibid. Here McAdams references an 1824 conversation between Thomas Jefferson and Daniel Webster on the eve of the presidential election where Jackson first stood as a candidate; the one in which he secured the majority of the 'popular vote' but did not reach the necessary threshold of 'electoral votes'. The election was thus decided by the House of Representatives: Henry Clay's supporters voted for Jackson's rival John Q. Adams in exchange for Clay becoming Secretary of State, in turn denying Jackson the presidency.

66   Biographies of Jackson have failed to identify a precise birthplace.

67   Dan P. McAdams, 'The Mind of Donald Trump', *The Atlantic*, June 2016.

4

Europa infelix – Brexit

If this Big Bang shook up the political, social and cultural land-scape of the West's leading power, it came after we had already heard loud creaking noises on the other side of the Atlantic. These noises came not only from those European countries where democracy was recently restored (or ones making their first approach to democracy) like Hungary and Poland, but also the French–German–Italian 'triangle' at the origins of the European project. The noises also owed to a structural collapse in America's own European alter ego: the United Kingdom, the very country where modern politics was born. There, too, an unexpected 'political geography' had emerged. This landscape had, so to speak, remained hidden behind the now well-worn mask of the traditional two-party system; now, one midsummer night, it made its dramatic entrance with a theatrical flourish, with all the disruptive force of the new populism. It appeared with hybrid traits and in an unconventional language, given both its temporal conflicts (nostalgia wrapped up with anxiety about change) and its moral convulsions (the combination of pride and fear, or of community feeling and stinginess). Above all else, it exhibited a visceral counterposition of those on top and those below. The divide cut horizontally through the two political parties that had monopolised the British political arena since time immemorial; and it eviscerated both.

The British earthquake

On the eve of the vote, it had rained in London and South East England as on few occasions in living memory. The weather remained bad throughout the day of 23 June. All the opinion polls indicated a stable lead for Remain,[1] and bookmakers were offering Remain at 1/7 and Leave at 4/1:[2] the sign of their near-absolute certainty that Remain would win. Even the count that evening began reassuringly enough; whoever went to bed at midnight could still have imagined the UK would remain the EU's twenty-eighth member. But, during the night, both the weather and the vote changed, and on the morning of 24 June, as magnificent sunlight beamed down on London, a contrite David Cameron emerged from 10 Downing Street to acknowledge the defeat and announce his own resignation. Leave had won with

---

1　The YouGov poll for *The Sunday Times* gave Remain a one point advantage over those who backed leaving the EU – 44 per cent to 43 per cent – though there was also a sizeable number of undecideds; Survation gave Remain a three-point advantage (45 per cent to 42 per cent).

2　These are the figures for PaddyPower and Bwin. SkyBet offered 2/13 and 3/1. William Hill, 'the UK's biggest bookmaker', had taken £20 million in bets already almost two weeks before the vote: it estimated that 71 per cent 'of betters' had bet on Brexit, but 73 per cent 'of the money' had backed Remain. This meant that while the small betters were oriented toward Brexit, those investing big amounts were 'against saying goodbye to the EU'. Of the £28.7 million taken by Betfair.com as of 10 June, £22.1 million was 'bet on staying in the EU'. See Antonio Atte, 'Brexit: le quote dei bookmakers', forexinfo.it, 23 June 2016.

51.9 per cent of the vote, with Remain at only 48.1 per cent. A very high proportion of eligible voters had turned out to vote – six points higher than the turnout at the previous general election, and a stunning figure for a referendum. Over 33.5 million citizens, or 72.2 per cent of the population, voted; those who backed Brexit prevailed by 1,269,501 votes.

But the overall data tells us little. Here, too, the colours on the map are rather more telling. In the British referendum, unlike in the US election, the map was coloured in orange and blue. But these colours still speak the same language and show fundamentally the same phenomenon: a vote that is more 'geographic', so to speak, than political, more governed by territory than by ideology. We can see this right away when we look at Scotland, in a uniform orange (the colour of Remain) and, to its left, Northern Ireland almost the same, while down below large swathes of England are coloured blue (where Leave won) with the only prominent orange spots being Greater London and a few blobs here and there representing some of the cities. Indeed, Leave won by a much greater margin in England, by almost six percentage points (53.3 per cent to 46.7 per cent) than in the United Kingdom as a whole, while in Scotland Remain won by an enormous margin (62 per cent to 38 per cent) and there was also a clear gap in Northern Ireland (55.8 per cent to 44.2 per cent). This tells us not only that the United Kingdom does not consider itself (to varying degrees) part of the European Union, but that it is not all that united in itself. Here was a change in the landscape – a 'genetic mutation', we could say – in a country considered the world's most stable democracy. This was certainly no business as usual, no occasional mishap.

Again, here, the media was dramatically taken by surprise and reacted with a mix of fear and amazement. Above all, of vertigo, almost a kind of *horror vacui*. The term most present across the newspaper titles was 'Out'; cast out, like those who find themselves suspended in the void. In some instances used as a one-word headline, vividly standing alone, as on the front page of Canada's *Calgary Sun*, where it appeared in block capitals against the backdrop of a gigantic Union Jack. More often it appeared as part of the expression 'WE'RE OUT', as in the *Daily Mail* and a dozen other tabloids and weeklies. Or else in more threatening form, as in the case of the *Daily Record*: 'Be afraid, be very afraid . . . we're on our way OUT!', with a dazed Boris Johnson's face as the backdrop. The other recurrent term was 'NOW' with a question mark, like in the *Kurier*, in which the text 'AND NOW?' appeared over the face of a terrorised citizen. Or as in the *Daily Mirror*: 'So what the hell happens NOW?' The more solemn *Times* went for the seismic 'Brexit Earthquake' and *The Wall Street Journal* the epochal 'Historic Elections', while the *Guardian* chose the gloomy 'Over. And Out'.

Almost all of 'the people who count' around the world had rallied behind Remain: 'Europol, MI5, MI6 and GCHQ, Goldman Sachs and J.P. Morgan, the United States, Australia and Canada, Tony Blair, John Major and Bob Geldof . . .'[3] along with NATO and the White House, the main Premier League clubs and prominent footballers, David Beckham in the lead,[4] the 'mother' of Harry Potter J.K. Rowling as well as John le Carré, the greater part of the TV and cinematic jet set, from the

---

3   Sarah Jones, 'Who voted for Brexit?', in *Commonware*.

4   In a Facebook post he wrote 'We live in a vibrant and connected world where together as a people we are strong. For our children and their children we should be facing the problems of the world together and not alone.'

Slumdog Millionaire director Danny Boyle to the *X Factor* creator Simon Cowell, as well as an array of actors and actresses from Jude Law and Emma Thompson to Dominic West and Benedict Cumberbatch,[5] the sculptor and star architect Anish Kapoor, the designer Vivienne Westwood, Elton John and Franz Ferdinand (the band), Nobel Prize winners such as Peter Higgs (who discovered the boson) and the cosmologist of 'black holes' Stephen Hawking, billionaires such as the Virgin boss Richard Branson[6] and top managers such as John Kampfner, chief executive of the Creative Industries Federation. Rather fewer names were behind Leave, including Joan Collins and Michael Caine (who explained that the United Kingdom should not be 'dictated to by thousands of faceless civil servants'), the *House of Cards* creator Michael Dobbs and the father of *Downton Abbey* Julian Fellowes, and some questionable role models such as Formula 1 boss Bernie Ecclestone. So, we can understand the disbelief and the shock at the verdict that came from the ballot box, just as would later happen in America with the 'impossible' election of Donald Trump.

---

5   They were among 282 figures who signed a letter in support of the Remain campaign, published in the *Daily Telegraph* on 19 May 2016 ('Letters. Actors, artists and writers look in the mirror and see a future in *The* EU'). They wrote, among other things, that if Brexit won, this would make each Briton 'an outsider shouting from the wings' and that leaving the EU would be 'a leap into the unknown for millions of people in the UK'. See also 'Celebrities including John le Carré and Keira Knightley back the pro-EU campaign', *The Daily Telegraph*, 10 May 2016.

6   Massimo Malpica, 'Brexit, cosí anche i vip si dividono a colpi di spot', *Il Giornale*, 22 June 2016; 'I vip e la Brexit: da Beckham a J.K. Rowling chi è per il "remain" ', *La Stampa*, 22 June 2016.

More maps. More 'cleavages'

Yet the amazement, the disconcert and the discomfort – in many cases, the genuine consternation – of the 'big media' and the 'powers-that-be' is not the only analogy that can be drawn between the British and American votes. As has been noted, there are also strong similarities in terms of the territorial distribution of the vote, which become particularly clear when we take a closer look 'on the ground' so to speak. Here, too, the 'uncomfortable' vote at odds with the mainstream opinion occupied a great deal more territory (if in less densely populated areas) than that in which the more predictable and 'conformist' choice won: Leave prevailed in 263 voting areas out of 382 – two-thirds of the total, leaving 119 to Remain – with the effect that, on the map, the blue, representing Brexit, covers the whole of England. The spread of one colour across the map is much more impressive, and suggests a much wider lead than the simple numerical data and the real gap between the 'Yes' and 'No' distribution of the vote would justify.

Rural areas and, once again, small provincial centres particularly clearly sided with Leave, in some cases with large majorities. Leave scored its biggest margin over Remain (almost half a million votes) in the Midlands, the great strip cutting across the island horizontally from the eastern county of Lincolnshire to the western counties of Herefordshire and Shropshire, where the old Kingdom of Mercia once prospered – a vast extension of hills and plains with a population density of 353 inhabitants per km^2. Boston, Lincolnshire, a small port town 100 miles north of London along the East Coast, was the voting area with the highest percentage for Leave, with a crushing 75.6 per cent majority. Remain, conversely, generally won the metropolitan areas (but not all of them) and, most importantly, did so by a very clear margin in Greater London. Here, with eight and a half million inhabitants concentrated in a relatively small space (about a twentieth the size of the Midlands, but with a population density of 5,223 residents/km^2) there was a 750,000-vote margin over Leave. And it was in the geographical centre, the inner-city boroughs of Lambeth and Hackney, that the 'Yes' to Europe scored its top results, with a resounding 78.5 per cent of the vote.

Yet the antithetical positions of town and country was not the only significant division that proves instructive in analysis of the British vote. In no other vote – including the American election – has the geographical cleavage been so deeply entwined with a social one, almost to the point of them merging (and indeed, things could not be much different in the homeland of the first Industrial Revolution). Voting 'No' to 'this Europe' were not only the isolated countryside areas resentful of the centre, with their low education levels and even poorer access to accurate information, but also many medium and large cities: the ones with the deepest industrial roots, and above all the areas with the greatest social suffering, hit hardest by the decline of manufacturing and the old economy. Essentially, the ones that continue to inhabit the 'lower levels' of a society undergoing overwhelming transformation. It is telling that Boston, once a flourishing Hanseatic port, has now been reduced to a rundown centre for the transformation of agricultural produce, with 31 per cent of its adult inhabitants classed 'clinically obese' (the highest obesity rate of any town in the UK, itself providing an indirect indicator of material deprivation). And it is worth reflecting on the fact that, in the Midlands, where Leave won by such a large margin, there are also major urban centres like Birmingham and Wolverhampton, as well as the so-called Black Country, the heart of English industry from the early nineteenth century, with its coal mines, foundries and steel mills.

The mirror image of this was reflected by the part of the population that has most benefited from the new economy overwhelmingly voting for Remain. This is the population distributed along the fast lanes of finance, communication, the so-called 'creative industries', the advanced tertiary and quaternary sectors, connected and interconnected in the open networks of globalisation. The people, indeed, on the 'higher levels'. A short video clip – no more than thirty seconds or so – broadcast by the BBC on 24 June portrayed a typical representative of the English working class, a man in his fifties with a check shirt, grey hair and a bulging stomach, wearing a yellow hardhat and a hi-vis jacket, in a typical central London street. Standing at the foot of an imposing glass-and-steel skyscraper, he looked up to the sky and the top of the tower, explaining to the reporter that 'them up there voted Remain, us down here voted Leave'. Meaning, this divide existed also in Greater London.

Indeed, if we look more closely at the result, breaking down the vote within the London urban area and its thirty-three boroughs, we see that this vote was anything but homogeneous. We see that in the capital the geographic cleavage had less effect than what we would once have called the 'class' divide: namely, one's position within the complex, changing and changeable (but also ruthless) selection mechanism that is the valorisation process. And if the boroughs that have benefited from the networks of finance and communications gave a 'Yes' to Remain as big as their inhabitants' incomes, the others, beyond the edge of Inner London and the circuit fed by the flywheel of financial circulation – the boroughs where they store industrial waste – answered with a likewise noisy Leave.

Like the aforementioned cases of Lambeth and Hackney, Wandsworth and Southwark also gave Remain among its strongest support nationally. Wandsworth is a residential area inhabited above all by established professionals attracted by its very low council tax rates, many of whom (49 per cent) are single, have high educational levels (56 per cent have at least one degree). Southwark is defined in the guides as a 'trendy and vibrant neighbourhood full of attractions', and has the London Eye (a giant wheel with panoramic views over the city) at its centre and the Tate Modern and Design Museum nearby. It is a textbook example of the gentrification process. With its massive urban restructuring operations, this process has attracted a very well-off population while pushing out less wealthy, or indeed decidedly poor inhabitants, who have to head off for cheaper areas. And the City and Westminster, boroughs steeped in economic and political power, naturally also voted Remain. But, as soon as we reach Bexley – another area on the banks of the Thames, but this time in 'outer London' on the south-eastern edge of the city, just like its 'twin' on the opposite side of the river, Barking and Dagenham – Remain received just 37 per cent of the vote. And in Havering, a typical suburb of an urban industrial periphery, a commuter borough built around the great Ford car plants, and later the site of new flows of migration and fresh poverty, Leave rocketed to 70 per cent!

Symmetrical and polarised identikits

The numbers and their socio-geographical distribution essentially confirm the concise identikit of typical voters that Sarah Jones sketched out right after the result. In her 26 June piece for the alternative news platform *Commonware* she focused on the opposite ends of the scale:

The typical Remain voter was a Scottish female university educated woman in her twenties who supported the Green party and had a high managerial, administrative or professional position. The typical Leave voter was a skilled male manual worker from East Anglia, who was over sixty years old, left school at 16 and supported UKIP.

An analysis of voting patterns makes it possible to refine this image further, adding more detail to this portrait, but does not alter its essential features.[7] It tells us, indeed, that the greatest concentrations of Remain supporters (above the national average) were to be found among full-time students, 72.6 per cent of whom opted for Leave, followed by those with degrees or postgraduate education (58 per cent and 64 per cent respectively), those belonging to the socio-economic group AB (Higher & intermediate managerial, administrative, professional occupations – 56.2 per cent),[8] Londoners (55.3 per cent), those who had taken at least one foreign holiday in the last three years, and full-time workers (51 per cent). Conversely, Leave was especially overrepresented among those without a formal education, 76.8 per cent of whom opted to quit the EU. Then came older Britons aged over fifty-five (64.8 per cent), pensioners (63.8 per cent), those belonging to the socio-economic groups C2 (Skilled manual occupations; 61.7 per cent) and DE[9] (semi-skilled & unskilled

7   My own interpretation of the voting intentions recorded by Populus and summarised in *The Remain Index* and *The Leave Index*.

8   AB is the top social grade in the ONS (UK Office for National Statistics) classification produced on the basis of an algorithm developed by the members of the MRS (Census and Geodemographics Group).

9   C2 and DE are the third and fourth social grades in the ONS classification.

manual occupations, unemployed and lowest grade occupations; 59.6 per cent), those who did not continue their education beyond secondary school (60.7 per cent), those who had not taken a foreign holiday over the previous three years (59.7 per cent) and those who rent Housing Association properties, i.e. those who cannot afford housing at market prices (57 per cent).

A few months after the vote, in October 2016, three researchers from the University of Warwick published a study on the composition of the Leave electorate[10] and in particular the motivations for their vote. Their study was based on sophisticated methodology and a mass of empirical data drawn from all of the UK's 380 local authority areas, thus allowing electoral behaviours to be cross-referenced with the social and structural characteristics of each local area. The research concentrated in particular on various 'items' or 'key drivers', meaning the indicators that were likely to influence the electoral preferences of different groups of citizens (for instance, their political affiliation, immigration status, economic conditions, cuts in public spending and tax credits, education levels, and working conditions) in the attempt to determine the 'predictive value' of each of these factors. This study is particularly interesting in that it uses a 'counterfactual' approach to measure how a change in these circumstantial conditions could have altered voting patterns (such that would, for instance, shift support from Leave to Remain and produce a different outcome).

The results are extremely telling, both at the descriptive level and in terms of the political conclusions to which they lead. The

---

10   Sascha O. Becker, Thiemo Fetzer and Dennis Novy, 'Who Voted for Brexit? A Comprehensive District-Level Analysis', *Working Paper Series*, no. 305. The University of Warwick, October 2016.

first thing that becomes clear is that political affiliation or, more generally, the way voters behaved in previous electoral contests, had a salient effect only for the voters for one party, indeed one 'invisible' in Parliament. This was Nigel Farage's UK Independence Party (UKIP) – the real 'stone guest'[11] of British politics, which, it should not be forgotten, had achieved its best ever result at the European elections in 2014, knocking the Labour and Conservative parties into second and third place. That result also owed to the proportional system used in the European elections; in parliamentary elections, UKIP has always been thwarted by the First Past the Post system, which hands a total victory in each constituency to the first-placed candidate, with nothing for those who come second or below.[12]

The support for Leave almost directly reflects the map of UKIP's strongest areas in that European election[13] (a sort of revenge, as this widespread expression of dissent and malaise, obstructed from the UK Parliament, again raised its head). For the big two parties (which, lest we forget, both declared for Remain – or at least, their leaderships took this stance), there was a minimal or non-existent correlation between the referendum result and their respective areas of strength: the distribution of voting areas in favour of Leave and Remain was independent of

---

11   A character in Molière's tragic play *Don Giovanni*, then adopted in Mozart's opera and Pushkin's tragedy: the stone guest is the statue of the man killed by Don Giovanni, who then leads him to hell at the end of the final act.

12   'Due to Britain's first-past-the-post voting system UKIP is otherwise hardly represented in national UK politics', Becker et al., 'Who Voted for Brexit?', p. 58.

13   'Understanding the UKIP vote share is crucial for understanding the vote in favour of Brexit', ibid., p. 22.

the greater or lesser concentration of votes for these parties in the last general election, even if surveys on the eve of the vote recorded a greater inclination for Remain among the Labour electorate and an advantage for Leave among Conservative voters. This was further confirmation, if one were needed, of the crisis of the traditional 'political cultures' and the increasing volatility of their respective voter bases, which are ever less bound by loyalty and respect for ties of belonging, and ever readier to desert the traditional parties.

The researchers also note that the distribution of the vote in the previous British referendum on staying in Europe had no 'predictive value' for the 2016 vote. Back in that 1975 referendum, 67 per cent of voters responded positively to the then-ruling Labour Party's campaign to remain in the Common Market. The map of that vote shows Remain winning almost everywhere (only the Hebrides, the islands far off the north-west coast of Scotland close to the Highlands, voted predominantly for Leave), with the brightest colours (indicating a greater than 65 per cent vote for Leave) across the whole of England, and paler ones (slightly above 50 per cent) in Scotland and Northern Ireland: the exact opposite of what happened in 2016. This says a lot about the deep transformations – the violent changes – that have matured in recent years in the British electorate's perceptions of Europe and its own political identity. And so, too, about how far the image that the EU has given of itself and its governance model must have moulded prevailing opinion in the United Kingdom.

The research does not deny the effect of immigration – a key issue in the referendum campaign, and an especially emotive one – in shaping the vote (and necessarily so). But immigration had such an effect within what was a rather more complex context than we might imagine, indeed a seemingly contradictory one. In fact, immigration was a significant 'key driver' in the referendum only with reference to the migration patterns from Eastern European countries who joined the EU between 2004 and 2013. It is an almost 'inert' or insignificant indicator when we look at migration patterns 'from older EU states or non-EU countries', i.e. the fifteen 'founder' members of the EU, and the migration from non-European countries, however massive, that is driving such strong 'populist' waves on the European continent. Moreover, the reaction to immigration seems to have been a greater driver of the Leave vote in the areas that are less directly (and materially) affected by immigration – the ones in which migrants make up a lower proportion of the overall population, or are even totally absent. This is a fine demonstration of the difference between 'feelings of alarm' and a 'real threat' and how much 'fear' influences and distorts the mechanisms of action and reaction in the political context.

Economic and socio-economic variables had a largely straight-forward effect: Leave was particularly strong in areas with a greater concentration of manufacturing (relatively more than in those areas where 'construction' and 'services' are most prevalent), in the areas where employment has grown in this sector in the last decade, and especially in manufacturing areas that are most dependent on imports and exports to and from European markets. Naturally, the education levels of the populations concerned – themselves a symptom of well-being or deprivation, or, in any case, a measure of socio-economic status – also had an impact. Working conditions had a particularly significant effect: the inclination for Leave was highest where wage levels were lowest and the type of work expected was worst, while Remain was stronger wherever conditions were better. The report tells us that 'a stronger increase in that variable [a higher median hourly pay since 2005 to 2015] is associated with a lower vote Leave share, consistent with the narrative that those 'left behind' were more likely to vote Leave.[14]

Unemployment was also a strong driver for Leave, while levels of self-employment or labour market participation had little notable impact. Leave secured considerably higher votes than average in areas where there was a high level of unskilled workers or workers with low education levels, as well as those in which employment in these layers of the workforce has grown in recent decades, while this inclination was weaker in those areas with higher qualification levels.[15]

But by far the most important indicator in terms of the distribution of the vote – if for nothing other than the fact that it is more dependent on the choices that stem from governance – concerns the provision of public services and policies for 'balancing the public accounts'. There is a strong 'positive correlation' between Leave and the voters living in rented council housing; those who live in council areas in which cuts in local public spending have been particularly sharp (in general, meaning less socially and economically well-off areas); and, particularly clearly, among the voters who face a more than sixty-two-day waiting time for essential medical treatment.[16] Conversely, Leave was less

---

14   Ibid., p. 25.

15   What the researchers call a 'surprising' exception is the fact that the Leave vote is also high in those areas which have seen fastest growth in high-skilled employment in the last decade. They tend to interpret this vote as a reaction to an accelerated demographic dynamic and, connected to this, greater pressure on housing and public services (ibid.).

16   One of the indicators used by the authors of the study was cancer patients' waiting time for their first surgery, after they had first been seen by a doctor, taking sixty-two days as a threshold.

favoured in areas with a high proportion of public-sector work-ers, itself indicating the continuing 'availability of public services and public jobs' and those with a higher proportion of commuters who work in London (so-called 'city users') who evidently belong to higher (and more secure) layers of the labour market and are in general better able to afford the high cost of services.

This, moreover, is the front on which the report tends to go beyond being merely descriptive and offer more criticisms and proposals. The most telling result of its 'counterfactual analysis' (which consists of testing what result could theoretically have been obtained if one or more circumstantial variables had been altered or removed entirely) is that even a small change in 'social policies', devoting even a small extra proportion of resources to 'public services' and the health service, could have eaten up a decisive share of the Leave vote and shifted the balance in favour of Remain. It would have been difficult, and in some cases impos-sible however, to change some of the structural factors influenc-ing the vote (age, education levels, workplace skill levels, expo-sure to transnational flows). As for immigration, any decisive shift would have required a massive correction of migration patterns which would have been impossible to achieve while also respecting human rights and existing EU labour market rules. But even a modest taming of budget cuts and, in particular, cuts in social spending, would have sufficed to 'shift' enough votes to push Leave under 50 per cent[17] (even reducing cuts by just 10 per cent, equivalent to £41 per person – the average total annual cuts averaged £448 per head – would have been sufficient to achieve this). This suggests that had the austerity policies shared by the governing parties and preached by Europe itself only been applied

---

17   Ibid.

less stubbornly and drastically, it would have been possible to avoid the 'British earthquake' (although there would have remained a serious reservoir of malaise and anger, which would have probably been ready to explode again if it found the opportunity to do so).

Between fear and fear

What lay behind the polarisation of the British referendum, then, was not 'political cultures' that had already clustered together. It was not driven by hardened and stable identitarian blocs, or by loyal electorates massed in solid political containers. No: there was a diffuse mood and a generalised sense of discontent (or instability). Above all, there was a fragmented society that struggled to find the words, the language, to express and identify itself. These, indeed, are the characteristics of the 'new generation' of populism that we face today. The cohorts that supported the opposing fronts in this battle are not cohesive or internally coherent. They were two constellations of heterogeneous figures and groups (two rabbles), sometimes riven by internal contradictions.

The Leave campaign especially played on the question of immigration and the threatening image of the country being invaded by Turkish hooligans and Polish plumbers (the photograph of a stream of refugees, on the march, was used as a propaganda weapon evoking atavistic terrorists). It also played on the cost of EU membership (its website claimed that the £350 million that the UK pays to the EU each week could instead be used for hospital building, to pay 8,000 new police officers, or to build ten schools a week). It appealed to voters' feeling of resentment faced with a plethora of privileged and arrogant bureaucrats (the European technocracy), and to their mounting fears of losing control over their borders and their own fate. Indeed, this was defined a 'Campaign of Fear'.

For its part, the Remain side raised the spectre of ruin and impoverishment in the unfortunate eventuality that Leave did win the referendum. The country would be abandoned by global capital; the City of London would be marginalised; and the UK would lose all the privileges that derive from being at the centre of globalisation, as well as the credibility it enjoys among the world's leaders and their respective populations. It emphasised the special advantages that the UK had negotiated with the European Commission in the past. It highlighted the fact that the 'refugees' would continue to crash in the distant waters of the Mediterranean; in any case, the barrier would hold at Calais. One video used by Remain supporters had a particular impact, showing the jeweller Alex Munroe explaining that, given that most of his business was with EU countries, a victory for Leave would force him to lay off a considerable share of the one hundred people he employed in London and Birmingham. This was a good encapsulation of the sentiments that drove the opponents of Leave. We could call it a 'Campaign of Greed'.[18] And it, too, was also a 'Campaign of Fear'.

But if 'fear' appeared on both sides of the barricades, and if fear was the real, and only, common denominator in a referendum that, by the very nature of the instrument used, was meant to measure the 'nation's sentiments', then this means that something was deeply broken. Something had broken in the essential foundations of social cohesion.

Indeed, if we take a closer look at each side, it is difficult to find elements serving as the glue for either of them – the motives for a

---

18   'Fear vs. Greed – the Real Candidates in the Brexit Referendum' is the title of an article by Roberto Savio published in *The World*, 18 June 2016.

collective, common action. Rather more striking is the wide distribution of positions within each respective camp. Here, we see the forced cohabitation of diverse figures and groups distant from each other in terms of both their political cultures and their personal and collective biographies. We see this in the case of Brexit's enemies, with Labourites and Conservatives forced into a common front, from David Cameron (who, making the worst mistake of his life, actively chose to hold the referendum) to Jeremy Corbyn (who seemed to find the referendum rather a burden, and was evidently ill at ease during it). Both of them were compelled to march together with one another and against a sizeable section of their own bases. And then there were the leaders of the pack in the City of London, the bosses of the financial markets, in a common front with the young millennials who faced uncertain futures, despite the Erasmus stays on their CVs. All of these forces devoted themselves to resisting the xenophobic impulses of their opponents' propaganda while also paying tribute to the steps the oligarchies in Brussels and Berlin had made to limit migration; speaking of the peace that had been guaranteed by the great European project, they simultaneously closed their eyes to the wars that had been tolerated and, in some cases, triggered, immediately outside EU borders.

The same was true on the side of those who wanted to say goodbye to Europe. Boris Johnson, the champion of English 'nativism', was in fact born in New York; his DNA carries the traces of infinite multi-ethnic ancestors from Ottoman Turks to Russian Jews, Frenchmen and Germans. He mimicked plebeian language and common behaviour and lost no opportunity to vaunt his disdain for the ruling political class and its breeding, despite having himself studied at Eton (where he was a classmate of Cameron's) and Oxford University and been Shadow Education Minister under Cameron's leadership between 2005 and 2008. He whipped up the unskilled workers worried by competition from migrants and called for more barriers to entry, but at the same time softened up voters of Asian background with the argument that halting migration from Eastern Europe would help allow their family members to come over from their home countries. Similarly, Nigel Farage (who lost no opportunity to contrast himself to Johnson) sharply criticised a 'society based only on money' and the dominance of finance, even though he made his own fortune as an exchange broker in the City, working for powerful firms like Lyonnais, Refco and Natexis Metals, and even though he began political life among the ranks of the Conservative Party.

Of the two, it is Farage who best incarnates the figure of the twenty-first century populist. It was he who, five days after the vote that marked both the culmination of his own career and a watershed in the European project, upbraided the Brussels parliament in brazenly mocking tones, with a highly effective speech in which he reminded his dumbfounded colleagues from the other twenty-seven countries that any slip-up in the UK's exit from the EU would do 'more harm to you than us'. Looking across the rows of seated MEPs he disdainfully commented that 'virtually none of you have ever done a proper job in your lives'. And it was again Farage who, throughout his seventeen years in this parliament, frontally and personally attacked the various representatives of the European institutions as bureaucrats and oligarchs, inhuman, irresponsible and bankrupt. On one occasion, looking him straight in the eyes, he told then European Council president Count Herman Achille Van Rompuy that he had 'all the charisma of a damp rag and the appearance of a low-grade bank clerk'.[19]

---

19 On 24 February 2010, commenting on the inauguration speech given by Van Rompuy upon his appointment as President of the European Council.

He made a frontal attack on European Commission President Barroso for having maintained a personal friendship with the Greek billionaire Spiros Latzis – lavishly financed with public funds, with the EU's approval – and for having enjoyed a gold-plated vacation on Latzis's yacht. And he did the same against the French commissioner Jacques Barrot, guilty of having diverted public funds into his own party's coffers. All this in the practised style of the grand prosecutor.

When, in July 2015, the Eurogroup and the European Commission conducted an astonishingly fierce and stubborn vendetta against Greece – a country guilty of opposing the lethal austerity policies that had been imposed upon it, and having held a referendum to say no to these exactions – it was Farage who issued the sharpest *j'accuse* before an impotent and supine European Parliament. He did this in the name of respect for the dignity of the Greek people and its democratically expressed will. He said that the deal – in reality, a Diktat – imposed on Greece showed that 'national democracy and the membership of the Eurozone are incompatible'.[20] This was not the first time that Farage had denounced the European Commission for sacrificing Greece. In a previous intervention at the European Parliament in Strasbourg on 16 November 2011 he had spoken of how:

> When Mr Papandreou got up and used the word 'referen-dum', you, Mr Rehn, described it as 'a breach of confidence', and your friends here got together like a pack of hyenas,

---

20   Quoted by Ian Silvera, 'Greek bailout deal: Ukip and Greens unite against controversial agreement', *International Business Times*, 13 July 2015, ibtimes.co.uk.

rounded on Papandreou, and had him removed and replaced by a puppet government. What an absolutely disgusting spectacle that was.

In a subsequent intervention in the European Parliament, on 22 May 2012, Farage further elaborated:

> We need to recognise that a terrible mistake has been made. We must resolve to put it right. We have got to give people hope because out there now is absolute despair. We all remember Dimitris Christoulas, the 77-year-old former pharmacist who shot himself dead outside the Greek Parliament, but he is just one of a growing humanitarian disaster. There have been huge increases in suicides in Italy and in Greece, particularly by people running small businesses who cannot see a way out of the problem. Children are being left in increasing numbers outside the doors of churches because their parents cannot afford to feed them. Our leaders are too callous to listen and care. You can do something about this.

None of the representatives of the two main groups in the European Parliament – either the centrist European People's Party or even their colleagues in the social-democratic parties of the Party of European Socialists – raised a word of dissent against this outright 'social sadism'. No one in the EU political establishment had the foresight to see this, but the inhumane image the 'European oligarchies' projected during the Greek crisis had no little impact on feelings of distance and real popular hostility toward the EU institutions, which also found expression in the

UK referendum result. Marco D'Eramo hits the nail on the head when he writes that 'it was not Brexit that set the European Union in crisis, but the crisis in the European Union that prompted the drives to leave.'[21] D'Eramo cites, in support of this argument, a sharp letter published in the *London Review of Books* (a publication clearly on the Left) on 31 March 2016, in the middle of the UK referendum campaign, in which among other things we read that:

> The EU that Britain is a member of is the same EU that presided over the brutalisation of the Greek people. It is the same EU that is currently, with a little help from NATO, seeking to repel desperate refugees from Syria, Afghanistan, Eritrea and elsewhere. It is the same EU that is engaging in the secret negotiations surrounding the TTIP, CETA and TiSA trade deals, which are designed to strengthen the role of multinational corporations and undermine regulations that protect people from them. Socialists should make no apology for mounting an independent, internationalist campaign against the EU.[22]

---

21   Marco D'Eramo, 'Brexit, il mondo è caduto dalle nuvole', *Micromega online*, 1 July 2016. He has also written an important and far-reaching essay on populism, 'Populism and the new oligarchy', in *New Left Review*, no. 89, July–August 2013.

22   Joseph Choonara, London E11, 'Letters', *London Review of Books*, vol. 38, no. 7, 31 March 2016.

5

Europa infelix, 2 – France, Germany . . . and the Rest

Meanwhile, in the four months between the UK referendum and the US presidential election, other alarm signals had also been coming from Continental Europe. In October 2016, news arrived from France that incumbent president François Hollande, now nearing the end of his term, had hit historically low levels of public support: while he had never, in truth, been very popular, his approval rating now fell to just 4 per cent (at least according to the Cevipof Institute,[1] a highly authoritative pollster, which also noted that no other French president had ever registered such levels of unpopularity). Polls were also showing an exponential rise in Marine Le Pen's support in the run-up to the 2017 presidential contest, within reach of 30 per cent of the vote.

A few weeks before the news about Hollande, in mid-September 2016 a summit had been held in Bratislava upon mainly German initiative, with the aim of offering an edifying image of

---

1 The Centre de recherches politiques de Sciences Po, which has kept the same acronym from the name it had until 2003, Centre d'études de la vie politique française. It works under the oversight of the CNRS and the Fondation Nationale de Sciences Politiques.

the European Union and showing that it remained united even after the humiliation of Brexit. At the summit the governments of the so-called Visegrád Group (Hungary, Czech Republic, Slovakia, Poland), four countries which had for some time been what newspapers called 'upholders of a hard line on migrant reception and severe critics of the German "open door" policy',[2] presented a document sharply critical of European governance and which called for greater respect for national sovereignty. The document criticised the practice of 'bilateral' (meaning: Franco-German) summits, and in effect rejected the use of quotas for sharing out 'refugees'. It proposed, as an alternative, that each state should be able to accept them at its own discretion, voluntarily.

At the time of the summit, the Visegrád Group was led by Hungarian Prime Minister Viktor Orbán – an authentic old-style right-wing populist, or in truth, something of a fascist – who had just announced the construction of a new wall, armoured with barbed wire and sharp steel spikes, along the border between Hungary and Serbia. For Orbán, 'the border cannot be defended with flowers and teddy bears but with police, soldiers and weapons. A new barrier will be built with the most modern technical equipment, capable of stopping hundreds or thousands of people'.[3]

This genuine revolt, in a part of Eastern Europe that Germany in a sense considers its own 'backyard', was a slap in the face for Chancellor Angela Merkel. In recent months, she had suffered

---

2 Giovanni Masini, 'Migranti, Norvegia ed Ungheria alzano nuovi muri di frontiera', ilGiornale.it, 26 August 2016, ilgiornale.it.

3 'Migranti, Orban: costruiremo un altro muro per fermarli', affaritaliani.it, 26 August 2016.

heavy losses in state elections, not least a particularly bruising defeat in Pomerania, on the Baltic coast – the very state that had elected her to the Reichstag. In this *Land* contest, which took place at the beginning of September 2016, just a few days before the Bratislava summit, Merkel's party was overtaken by Alternative für Deutschland (AfD), a new 'populist' formation which here achieved an unexpected breakthrough. But, already in previous elections in the most diverse *Länder* – from wealthy Baden-Württemberg, in the south, to the more rural state of Saxony in central Germany, and even in Berlin – the AfD had proven an extremely dynamic and rising force.

The 'new front' in France

'And so Europe is panicking again'. Such was the 'Zero Hedge' website's remark on the news, splashed across the *Independent* on 20 November 2016, that Marine Le Pen had taken a 'huge lead' over her competitors in polling for the first round of the French presidential elections set for 23 April 2017.[4] For *The Independent*, she was on course to 'secure a surprise victory in the wake of the UK's Brexit vote and Donald Trump's US election win'.[5] The article cited a freshly published Ipsos poll, which set out five scenarios for the election (depending on which contenders emerged from the other parties' primaries); in each case, the study placed the Front National leader at the top of the standings on a solid 29 per cent, 8 points ahead of

---

4   Lucy Pasha-Robinson, 'Marine Le Pen takes huge lead over Nicolas Sarkozy in French first round presidential election poll', *The Independent*, 20 November 2016.

5   Ibid.

Sarkozy (if he had been the Républicains' candidate) and 15 ahead of Valls and Mélenchon.[6] These figures were similar to those given in a similarly structured Ifop poll.[7] In response, Bernard-Henri Lévy offered his own 'apocalyptic' comments to *The Telegraph*, according to which 'If Trump is possible, then everything is possible. Nothing, from now on, is unimaginable.'[8]

It should be said 'Zero Hedge' is a dubious, indeed controversial blog. Wikipedia says it 'has been classified as "alt-right", anti-establishment, conspiratorial, and economically pessimistic'. It is inspired by the film *Fight Club* and its critics suggest that it is overly pro-Russian. And these explosive, threatening polls ultimately proved mistaken – or in any case, became obsolete – when, in the months leading up to the beginning of the campaign, Emmanuel Macron and his En Marche! vehicle burst onto the stage and changed the script. But, doubtless, these signals emanating from the depths of the electorate gave some measure of the powerful upheaval that had come to a head in little more than five years, in the subsoil of a public opinion that had now become almost unrecognisable. If we consider that this support for Marine Le Pen, counting for almost a third of the electorate, was almost double her result in the 2012 contest (and, back then, her 17 per cent of the vote had already seemed high!) we get some idea of the powerful upheavals which seem

---

6   Ibid.

7   'If Trump is possible, then everything is possible. Nothing, from now on, is unimaginable'. See James Rothwell, 'Leading French philosopher: Marine Le Pen may win election as people have lost interest in whether politicians tell the truth', *The Telegraph*, 20 November 2016.

8   Ibid.

to have changed France's electoral geography, and the topography of the Front itself.

When Le Pen *père* – Jean Marie – founded the Front National in October 1972, it was a typical neo-fascist type microformation. It gathered together the nostalgists for all of France's past high points of reaction, from former collaborators of Pétain to former Poujadists, Catholic *intégralistes* and those 'repatriated' from *Algérie française* (the so-called *pieds-noirs* driven out of Algeria after France's defeat in its final, lost colonial war). So, too, *Action française*–style monarchists who raised the banners of anti-parliamentarism and nationalism, and the extra-parliamentary Right of *l'Ordre Nouveau* . . . In the first parliamentary elections in which it took part, in 1973, the Front got a paltry 0.5 per cent of the vote, and at the subsequent presidential elections in 1974 just 0.8 per cent. Only in the 1980s, after François Mitterrand's victory in the presidential elections spurred a strong anti-socialist and anti-communist reaction on the Right, did the Front begin its electoral rise, securing an 'exceptional' 11 per cent in the 1984 European elections and then almost 10 per cent in the 1986 French parliamentary contest.[9]

However, what we could call the 'first life' of Le Penism – Jean-Marie's version – made its real breakthrough with the 2002 presidential election, when he scored the enormous coup of reaching second place in the first round, edging out the Socialist candidate Lionel Jospin (by just over 200,000 votes; 16.9 per cent to 16.2 per cent). He then faced Jacques Chirac in the run-off, which Chirac won with an enormous 82 per cent majority. This

---

9 For a reconstruction of the Front National's history, see Valérie Igounet, *Le Front national de 1972 à nos jours. Le parti, les hommes, les idées*, Seuil, Paris, 2014.

owed to the iron rule of the 'second round', through which the electorate of the competitors defeated in the first round rallies behind the most similar candidate, against the other who is considered more distant or more unfavourable. But the most interesting data from this 2002 contest concerned the territorial distribution of the 'Le Penist' vote itself: the map produced by *Documentation française* shows two horizontal strips, one in the far north-eastern quarter of France, the other along the Mediterranean coast of the Midi, in the darkest colours (i.e., indicating the regions where Le Pen secured over 16 per cent of the vote), as opposed to a large grey area (where he secured between 10 and 16 per cent) in the central-eastern strip, and a large white splash (where he scored under 10 per cent) across the whole of central and western France, including the entire Atlantic coast. The areas coloured in an almost homogeneous black (which can be defined Jean-Marie le Pen's 'Main Geographical Stronghold') included Upper Normandy, Picardy and Lorraine, including part of Alsace, with Champagne-Ardenne in the middle; and, on the other side of the country, Provence-Alpes-Côte d'Azur (the PACA region) up to the Bouches-du-Rhône passing along the river Var.

This has prompted the so-called 'theory of two Fronts',[10] each of which has its own particular social as well as geographical connotations. According to this theory, the Front National draws its support from two distinct socio-demographic groups: the *Front du Sud* represents the regions where the party first took root, and continuity with the Poujadists of the 1950s and the post-Algerian legacy of the following decade; while the

---

10   Jérôme Fourquet, *Front du Nord, Front du Sud*, Ifop Focus no. 92, August 2013, Paris.

Front du Nord is the expression of a region with a greater working-class population and a *travailliste* tradition. The latter is a region in which the party has taken root more recently, and in which it has more of a protectionist and 'anti-capitalist' bent (in a sense, a more 'social' Front). The *Front du Sud*, by contrast, is more politically entrenched, drawing on the classical 'reactionary Right', is more on the side of the bosses, and reflects a social base largely composed of higher-income pensioners – former professionals and managers – traders, artisans and the self-employed.

For those who propose this theory, the differences between these two Fronts has continued to manifest itself over the medium term, and is expressed even in the most recent 'differences of positioning' between Marine Le Pen – more an expression of the *frontisme* proper to the north-east – and her niece Marion Maréchal Le Pen, the spokesperson of a southern *frontisme* deeply immersed in 'her' Vaucluse *département* and an attitude that is more *classiquement droitier*.

From the 'black fortresses' to all of France

Indeed, the distribution of the Front National vote in the 2012 presidential elections, when the candidate was again a Le Pen (this time, the daughter), would seem to corroborate the thesis that the Front's support continues to be drawn from these two traditional bases. After all, the Front's support was most concentrated in the same areas as before: again, the north-eastern quarter of France and a strip along the Mediterranean. But this is an optical illusion. Even the strength of support with which Marine Le Pen now attained third place was at least 1.5 million votes above the numbers with which her father had reached the run-off,[11] and there was also a jump in the party's overall percentage. The 'strongholds' displayed on the map in an off-black dark brown now represented first-round levels of support of above 21 per cent (5 points more than her father's 2002 score). They also had a greater geographical extension, for they now coloured an almost unbroken strip across the whole eastern part of France. Meanwhile, the areas represented in lighter or near-white hues now represented scores under 15 per cent, rather than 10 per cent as before. A Front that had now renewed itself – and this was not only a facelift – had begun its triumphant march toward the west.

Clearly, the last decade had not been in vain. And Marine Le Pen's attempt to 'de-demonise' the Front National – playing down its more nostalgic and explicitly neo-fascist aspects, sterilising its earlier Pétainist and anti-Semitic attitudes, and turning its original ideological and sectarian political aspects in a more social direction – had succeeded at least in part. Essentially, the daughter could not be accused of the same obscenities as her father, who had described the gas chambers as a mere 'detail in the history of the Second World War'[12] and participated in the Algerian War, in which he tortured prisoners. Rather, in her six years as a lawyer and member of the Paris Bar Association, she had spent her career defending human rights, including those of undocumented migrants. This did not stop her making the question of immigration and the fight against it a key part of the Front's programme, once she had taken over the leadership (in Lyons in 2010 she

---

11   In 2012, they secured 6,421,426 votes, compared to 4,804,713 in 2002.

12   For this reason, he was expelled from the Front in 2015, at his daughter's instigation, in a sort of family duel.

compared Muslims praying in the streets of France to a military invasion, similar to the German occupation of 1940). But this issue took something of a backseat compared to other questions she considered strategically important such as the radical critique of globalisation and finance capitalism; the attack on the European Commission's austerity policies and bureaucratic *dirigisme*, as she instead upheld a proud 'sovereigntyism'; and played on themes of deindustrialisation, unemployment and new forms of inequality.

Similarly, she pulled back on the Front's original homophobia, showing her more open and pragmatic stance on questions like the recognition of same-sex marriage and gay rights. In this sense, she was closer to the spirit of the *Front du Nord* than the *Front du Sud*, but this also had the strategic thrust of truly making the Front National a party 'for all the French', with slogans like *Au nom du peuple* ('In the name of the people') and *Les Français d'abord* ('Put the French first') or even *Oui! La France* ('Yes, France!'). Two years after that presidential contest, in the 2014 European elections the Front National came in first place with almost 25 per cent of the vote, defeating the moderate Right of the UMP by over four points and practically doubling the Socialists' tally as this party slumped to 13 per cent. In the *départementales* of March 2015, her candidates secured 572,102 votes more than they had in the previous year's European elections, and over 1.7 million more than they had in the 2012 parliamentary contest. In the 2015 regional elections, the Front's lists came top in the first round in 20,081 *communes*, as against 10,080 for the Union of the Right and 6,524 for the Union of the Left[13] (though

---

13   As of 1 January 2015, there were 36,658 *communes* in France, almost half the total number of local municipalities in the entire European Union.

the usual second-round effect meant that the Front did not secure even one regional presidency out of the seventeen contested).[14] In any case, this considerably redrew the French political map. As expert analyst Yves-Marie Cann observed, 'Election after election, the Front National wins new voters and expands its own core vote.' Thus, Cann described what he has defined as the 'Conquest of the West':[15] the march toward the 'new geography' of Marine Le Pen's party.

This same expression had also been used by Béatrice Giblin – a geographer, founder of the Institut français de Géopolitique at the Université Paris VIII, and editor of the prestigious journal *Hérodote* – in an article published in *Le Monde* entitled 'La nouvelle géographie électorale du Front National'. Here, Giblin remarked upon Marine Le Pen's decision to stand candidates in the greatest possible number of towns, from the March 2014 municipal elections onwards. She defined this as a 'strategy that had paid off', thanks to which the numerous hitherto empty spaces in the Front's political map had rapidly been filled in. Its lists reached at least 10 per cent, even in towns and territories in which it had never previously existed – thus confirming its *ancrage national*. Each fresh electoral map from this point onward showed that the Front National was spreading across the whole central area of France, including the Massif Central, and reaching all the way along the Atlantic coast, from Brittany to

---

14   However, the Front secured 358 regional and territorial councillors, as against 493 for *Les Républicains* (the name adopted by the former UMP, upon Sarkozy's instigation) and 355 for the Socialists.

15   Yves-Marie Cann, 'Vers une nouvelle géographie électorale? Ce que révèle la forte poussée du vote FN dans le Nord-Ouest et sur la façade atlantique', *Atlantico*, 28 October 2015.

Aquitaine, where the Le Pens had never previously laid roots. She added:

> In these results, there is doubtless one motivation common to the whole Front National electorate: rejection of the UMP and PS. For these voters, the exchange of power [between these two parties] has done nothing to change the situation. Unemployment, insecurity and immigration [continue]. Why not, then, vote for the party that truly wants to change politics entirely?[16]

This is, to some degree, a new spur to vote Front National – a mood, even. This itself corresponds to the change in the *lepéniste* electoral agenda (however partial), which has shifted in an ever more 'socially oppositional' direction. And this has lessened, if not entirely done away with, the one-time territorial polarisation (or at least segmentation) of the Front's electoral map.

Two other scholars of geopolitics and, in particular, the *lepéniste* electoral geography have arrived at similar conclusions. In the wake of the 2015 regional elections Joël Gombin and Sylvain Crépon observed that 'we need to deconstruct our pre-conceived ideas, if we are to understand the recomposition of the electorate that is now taking place.'[17] In particular, they consider the 'two Fronts' schema too reductive for describing a (now) more

---

16   Béatrice Giblin, 'La nouvelle géographie électorale du Front National', *Le Monde*, 27 March 2014.

17   Joël Gombin and Sylvain Crépon, 'Loin des mythes, dans l'isoloir', *Le Monde Diplomatique*, no. 134, April–May 2014. See also Joël Gombin, 'Les trois visages du vote FN', *Le Monde Diplomatique*, 1 December 2015 and, together with Cécile Marin, 'Géographie électorale de l'extrême droite', ibid.

complex political phenomenon. And some persistent myths also need pulling apart, for example the myth of a Front National fuelled – especially in the south – by a 'bourgeois and conservative', largely Catholic-traditionalist and nostalgic vote.[18] The authors tell us that such an image was justifiable until the beginning of the 1990s, but across the following quarter-century it has no longer applied. Indeed, it is precisely in the 'Catholic West', in Brittany and in the Vendée, that the Front has struggled most to add to its vote, even as it has grown across France. The fact is, the pair add, that since 2000 a polarisation has emerged among the *frontiste* electorate, with the elements of society that were already previously less present among its electorate ('managers and higher-level intellectual professions, intermediate levels of the public sector') tending to vote for it ever less, and the ones that were already most present ('blue-collar workers, supervisors, company technicians, sales clerks, the low-earning self-employed') ever more committed to voting Front National.[19] 'Some categories "oscillate" between the two', Gombin and Crépon add, namely 'those most exposed to the negative consequence of globalisation: engineers and white collar employees – especially white-collar employees! – that were previously less inclined to vote for Le Pen'.

In this reading, it is globalisation and its impact on French society (and indeed, societies across the West), combined with

---

18   Among the other myths that need undoing, Gombin and Crépon also mention the notion that the Front National is the beneficiary of a former Communist vote, especially in regions with a large population of blue-collar workers. In their view, this hypothesis is not confirmed by any analysis of shifts in voting patterns ('Loin des mythes').

19   Ibid.

the neoliberal policies that have accompanied it, that has shaken up the electoral map, reducing the geopolitical differences between the 'two Fronts' and most importantly extending the party's influence across all of France, and to social categories that were previously little present among its electorate, such as blue-collar workers.[20] Thus, 'the FN's electoral map' no longer corresponds 'to any form of historical legacy',[21] whether that of Poujadism, the colonial nostalgia of Tixier-Vignancourt's *Forces Nouvelles* or the reactionary soul of the grandchildren of Charles Maurras.

What most boosts the Front's propaganda today is the fact that a majority of French society is experiencing a general worsening of its living conditions; for these citizens, government policies and indeed the policies imposed by Europe seem to rub salt into the wounds. Of course, this has varying effects across different geopolitical areas: in the Nord, for example, but also in part of the Bouches-du-Rhône, 'industrial decline in a rural, blue-collar

---

20   For Cécile Marin, author of a series of cartographic works designed to deconstruct the main 'myths' surrounding the *frontiste* vote, 'The FN's large audience among blue-collar voters dates to the first half of the 1990s. Previously the *lepéniste* party had above all rallied a more bourgeois electoral clientele, especially among shopkeepers'. These myths include the claim – which has now become part of the common sense of the party – that the Front 'inherited' the old Communist vote after the end of the USSR and the crisis of the French Communist Party (PCF). Marin shows, on the basis of the electoral map, that 'there is neither a correlation between the geographic structure of the PCF and FN votes, nor a temporal coincidence between the decline of the former and the rise of the latter' (Cécile Marin, 'Non, le vote FN n'est pas immuable', *Le Monde Diplomatique*, no. 134, April 2014 (monographic issue devoted to the *Nouveaux visages des extrèmes droites*).

21   Gombin, 'Les trois visages du vote FN'.

context' feeds and sustains a reaction based on a 'social sovereign-tyism'; in western France, where the last two decades of the twentieth century and the first decade of the new century saw new industries being established, the population instead experiences the repercussions of the recession and the feeling of losing what was an only ephemeral wellbeing; meanwhile, in the south, where the economy is more linked to tourism, and a considerable mass of medium- and high-income pensioners live adjacent to areas with a high concentration of poorer citizens, it is the frustrations and fears connected to feelings of insecurity that count for most. Hence, the party has a 'complex' social composition and a hetero-geneous electorate, itself bringing out new lines of differentiation. There is no longer just a *Front du Nord* and a *Front du Sud* but also a *Front des Villes* in the towns and a *Front des Champs* in the countryside, a *Front des Immeubles* in the housing blocks and a *Front des Pavillons* for those in detached properties. A new Front National that seeks to become the party 'of all the French' offers these various different groups a 'differentiated ideological offer', calibrated according to the specificities of each given territory. But this is 'simplified', so to speak, by an issue that can emotionally activate all of these different Fronts: namely, the fear of immigrants. And so, too, by a strong 'social-populist discourse' – a discourse that is anti-Europe, anti-globalisation, anti-oligarchies, anti-bureaucratic and neo-chauvinist, but in a 'social' sense. This is used as an extraordinary 'means of removing the obstacles to electoral support among social groups that still accord some importance to the social question and have been *abandoned by the Left*'.[22]

---

22   Ibid. (my italics). The expression 'social-populist' is drawn from Gilles Ivaldi, 'Du néolibéralisme au social-populisme? La transformation du programme économique du Front national (1986–2012)', in Sylvain

It is telling that Marine Le Pen was one of the first political figures in the world to offer her congratulations to Donald Trump immediately after his election as president of the United States, explaining that 'with their vote the Americans have rejected the "status quo"'; and indeed, that she did the same in June 2016 immediately after the Brexit vote, with a message to the 'very brave' Boris Johnson and a press conference in Brussels to announce her intention to propose a similar referendum on Frexit in her own country. At the same time, her number two Florian Philippot enthusiastically tweeted: 'The freedom of the peoples always wins in the end! Bravo, United Kingdom. Now, our turn.' In the Front National's propaganda, the turning point in Britain marked 'the beginning of the end for the European Union'; the end of what Le Pen's party denounced as 'the Germans' Europe'.

After the 'trial by fire'

Marine Le Pen did not win the French presidential election. She was defeated by Emmanuel Macron, who secured a clear 66 per cent to 34 per cent majority in the second round. France did not join the United States and United Kingdom and form a 'triangle' of populisms in government in the countries key to the world order. Europe breathed an enormous sigh of relief.[23] This relief

---

Crépon, Alexandre Dézé and Nonna Mayer, eds., *Les Faux-Semblants du Front national. Sociologie d'un parti politique*, Presses de Sciences Po, Paris, 2015.

23 'Macron's victory was welcomed with a sigh of relief in Europe, where many saw it as a litmus test of strength for the populist insurrections around the continent', John Burn-Murdoch, Billy Ehrenberg-Shannon, Aleksandra Wisniewska and Aendrew Rininsland, 'French election results: Macron's victory in charts', *The Financial Times*, 9 May 2017.

was directly proportional to the great fear that had built up on the eve of the election, but it was only in part justified (and, indeed, only within a short-term perspective). A dispassionate analysis of the data makes it clear that, not only had the Front not been set back even a millimetre, but that it had greatly built on its previous advance. The 10,637,120 votes that Madame Le Pen secured in the run-off were almost double what her father Jean-Marie had won in 2002 (5,525,032) and 4,215,694 more than the number she had herself won in 2012, when she came third in the first round with 6,421,426 votes. This score was also 3,816,673 votes higher than the result the Front had attained (in what was, at the time, considered a triumph) in the 2015 regional election.

Notwithstanding the notable discrepancy between the final result and the polls on the eve of the vote (which had credited Marine Le Pen with 40 per cent of the vote before the disastrous TV head-to-head debate on 3 May) and the consequent disappointment of the Front's supporters, it is nonetheless impossible to 'hide the fact that since 2012 and indeed since 2002 there has taken place a spectacular advance in the Front National's vote'.[24] This was, indeed, observed from many quarters, though it was almost drowned out amidst the noise of the victors' fanfare. In reality the 'populist danger' in France has far from been erased, and one can recognise a certain realism in the Front National MEP who said on 8 May that 'to speak as a salesperson, we are eating up market shares at every election . . . The general trend is

---

24   Luc Rouban, 'Pour comprendre le vote Front national, La victoire d'Emmanuel Macron ne doit pas faire oublier le score réalisé par Marine Le Pen. Analyse du vote en faveur du parti frontiste depuis 2002', *The Conversation France*, lepoint.fr, 9 May 2017.

extremely favourable for us.'[25] Indeed, the numbers tell us that, notwithstanding the prohibitive conditions imposed by French electoral law in the second round (it is an almost iron law that in such a case the losing candidates' voters rally behind the candidate opposed to the more 'extreme' one) the Front National maintained its strength in its 'usual strongholds' (in the northeast, where it won in the Aisne and the Pas-de-Calais,[26] and on the Mediterranean coast where Marine Le Pen often ran Emmanuel Macron close), while also building its support in almost every region. This confirmed the Front's 'march to the West' and the tendency for its electoral geography to become ever more genuinely 'national'.[27] If we look at the Front's electoral map, based on different shades of grey, we can see that alongside two very dark, almost black patches in the north-east and along the Mediterranean coast, where Marine Le Pen's percentage on 7 May was above 40 per cent, there was a broad sweep of dark grey covering eastern France and a good part of the centre, where the Front's candidate scored over 30 per cent. The only light grey patches (where she took under 30 per cent of

---

25   Bruno Gollnisch (Front National MEP), 'Election 2017: How France voted, 8 May 2017', *Connexion*, 8 May 2017.

26   In the Aisne, Marine Le Pen won with 52.9 per cent of the vote, as she did in Pas-de-Calais with 52 per cent, while in the Ardennes, the Meuse, the Haute Marne and the Haute-Saône it was close to a tie. So, too, in the Var (where she scored 49.2 per cent), in the Vaucluse (46.6 per cent), in the Pyrénées Orientales (47.1 per cent), and in the Gard.

27   As summarised on europe1.fr's special page: 'Marine Le Pen maintains her strongholds in the north-east and south-east and can draw satisfaction from the roots sunk across the whole of France' ('Abstention record, vague Macron, score élevé du FN: le second tour de la présidentielle en cartes', 8 May 2017).

votes) were in the far north-west (the four *départements* of Brittany),[28] a few *départements* in the Massif Central (Puy-de-Dôme, Corréze, Aveyron) and, naturally, the Paris metropolitan area. In no *département* except Paris (and Hauts-de-Seine, in the same metropolitan area), did the Front get under 20 per cent!

This phenomenon is yet more visible in the maps depicting the first-round outcome. It is this vote that measures the real strength of each political force, its 'true' electorate. Particularly useful is the map that shows which candidate came first in each *commune*, filled in with the colours of the respective candidate (black for Le Pen, orange for Macron, red for Mélenchon (France Unbowed), pink for Hamon (Socialist Party) and blue for Fillon (Les Républicains)):[29] there is a striking concentration of black dots, making up an almost homogeneous blob across the north-eastern quarter of France (east of the Greenwich meridian and north of the 47th parallel, with the exception of the Île-de-France region around Paris), but also along the whole strip running from north to south across the part of France east of the 5th meridian. Then there is an only slightly thinner spread of black dots across the Midi, along the course of the river Garonne to its estuary onto the Atlantic, and in the central part of the country to the south-west of Paris. A distribution of colour which would suggest that from a geographical point of view at least Marine Le Pen 'occupied' (in the first round!) a larger swathe of territory than her competitors. To repeat, that does not imply that this is also the largest share of

28 Côtes-d'Armor (26.5 per cent), Ille-et-Vilaine (22.3 per cent), Morbihan 28.4 per cent), Finistère (22.7 per cent).

29 PopulationData.net. 'Atlas des populations et pays du monde, France – élections présidentielles 2017, 1er tour, 28 avril 2017', populationdata.net.

the electorate, for as we already saw with the examples of Trump's result in the United States and the Brexit referendum, the 'populist' offer prevailed in less densely populated regions,[30] even if over the widest total area.

The statistics for the first-placed candidate in each *commune* in the first round confirm that Marine Le Pen won in almost 19,000 (54 per cent of the 36,658) French *communes*[31] as against 7,000 for Macron (not much over 20 per cent).[32] She was 'let down' by metropolitan areas and the big cities, in particular Paris, where she did not come first in any *arrondissement*[33], but also Lyons,

---

30   'Thus between Paris with its 20,000 inhabitants/km^2 and Alpes-de-Haute-Provence with its 23/km^2 (6,925 km^2 for 160 000 inhabitants), the classic maps can give the impression that large pieces of territory and likewise large numbers of inhabitants have been won by this or that candidate. Thus while the FN candidate racked up votes in the East of France, the relative weight of these regions is less than that of Western *départements* which are less willing to vote for Marine Le Pen.' Pierre Breteau, 'Les résultats par département au second tour de la présidentielle 2017, rapportés à la population', LeMonde.fr, 8 May 2017.

31   In the second round Marine Le Pen held on to 9,194 of these 19,000 *communes* (Macron was first in 26,044). This was nonetheless a considerable total, confirming the Front's progress over time, especially if we consider that when Jean-Marie Le Pen reached the second round in 2002 he won only 34 *communes* ('In numbers: How the French voted (and how they didn't)', *The Local*, 8 May 2017, thelocal.fr).

32   'François Fillon [had to settle] for five thousand (16 percent) and Jean-Luc Mélenchon for around 3,500 (a little under 10 percent). The hapless Benoît Hamon had to settle for the very modest figure of sixteen communes – behind Jean Lassalle (seventy-eight)', Roger Martelli, 'X-Ray of a Shattered Vote', *Jacobin*, 5 May 2017.

33   Macron took thirteen of Paris's twenty *arrondissements* with his 34.83 per cent vote share, over 8 points over François Fillon, who won in five (the capital's *beaux quartiers*: the 6th (39.7 per cent), 7th (52.7 per cent)

Toulouse, Bordeaux, Nantes (where she came fifth, with scores between 7.1 and 9.3 per cent) as well as Lille, Strasbourg, Montpellier (where she came fourth), while she came second in Marseilles (behind Mélenchon) and Nice (behind Fillon). Conversely, she took the greater part of the rural *communes* (where she averaged over 25 per cent in the first round, almost 4 points better than her national tally) and in small towns,[34] following a familiar pattern which we had already seen with Trump's vote in the United States and with Brexit in the United Kingdom. Here, too, it was *la France profonde* – the France of the provinces, as against that of the urban centres, the France that stands distant from the capital and the poles of rapid communication and accelerated time – that handed the advantage to the populist candidate. The spread of the vote for the Front proved to be relatively autonomous of traditional political cultures and their territorial strongholds: it cut across them horizontally, so to speak, once again placing the centre–periphery and city–countryside cleavages over the one between Left and Right (the Front has, indeed, conquered numerous traditional Socialist strongholds).

8th (50.48 per cent), 17th (37.71 per cent) and 16th (58,45 per cent). Jean-Luc Mélenchon won in the working-class 19th and 20th *arrondissements* (30.69 per cent and 31.8 per cent respectively). Marine Le Pen scored just 4.99 per cent of the vote in Paris, less than in 2012 (6.2 per cent). In the second round Macron pulled off a landslide in every *arrondissement*: 93 per cent in the 2nd (Bourse), 3rd (Temple), 10th (Enclos-Saint-Lauren) and 11th (Popincourt); 92 per cent in the 9th (Opéra), 91 in the 6th (Luxembourg), and between 88 per cent and 90 per cent in all the others, except the 16th (Passy) where he scored 87 per cent.

34   Marine Le Pen achieved her best score in rural *communes* (43 per cent) and her worst in towns with populations over 100,000 (28 per cent) (Source: Ipsos/Sopra Steria).

The electoral geography is not the only way in which the French case resembles the American and British ones. As John Burn-Murdoch et al. observe, the socio-economic maps of the three 'electoral earthquakes'

are also marked by striking analogies. As in the case of the US vote for Trump and the British vote for Brexit, in the French presidential election the populist candidate found her highest concentration of support among the less-educated electorate (this could be considered 'the biggest single predictor of a vote for Ms Le Pen).[35]

This section of the electorate also held the lowest incomes, worked in manual jobs or were some other kind of wage earner (in both public and private sectors),[36] were among the social layers that subjectively feel a process of *déclassement*[37], were mainly concentrated in the areas with the highest rates of

---

35 Burn-Murdoch et al., 'French election results'. A graphic included in the article shows that Macron won with a very high score (84 per cent) 'in the top 10 per cent most educated communes'. But he secured his lowest score (53 per cent, 13 below his average) 'in the least educated 10 per cent of communes'. In this regard see also the Ipsos/Sopra Steria survey conducted on the eve of the second round and published on the day of the vote itself: '2ème tour présidentielle 2017: comprendre le vote des français'.

36 Ibid. 'Macron won 82 per cent among the 10 per cent of voters who live in areas with the lowest shares of blue collar jobs . . . Macron won 56 per cent [26 points under the average] among the 10 per cent of voters who live in areas with the highest shares of blue collar jobs.'

37 '56 per cent of those surveyed who think their condition is worse than their parents' was (at the same age) vote FN, as against 39 per cent of those who think their situation is similar and 31 per cent of those who think their situation is better.'

unemployment and de-industrialisation, and can be characterised by lower life expectancy.[38]

It is telling that the only professional category in which Marine Le Pen beat Emmanuel Macron in the second round, according to the Ipsos data, was blue-collar workers (among whom she scored 56 per cent).[39] Equally revealing is the fact that the duel between the two candidates was almost even-handed among voters with an education level below the *bac* (roughly equivalent to A-levels), while Macron won a landslide among top managers (82 per cent) and those with a three-year university degree or higher (81 per cent).[40] Again according to Ipsos, the vote for Marine Le Pen was highest among families with incomes at €1,250 a month or less (45 per cent, almost even with Macron) and then had a downward trend among higher income groups, with her lowest score of 25 per cent among those with incomes at €3,000 or higher.[41] In substance, Macron proved to be the candidate 'of the France which is doing well', and secured his best results 'among the most comfortably-off'; he appealed to an 'optimistic France which is doing fine and thinks that the young generation will do better

---

38   There is an almost total correlation between the vote for Macron and life expectancy (Macron's vote was below 50 per cent in *départements* where female life expectancy is eighty-two, and at its highest in those in which this figure rises above eighty-six). The 'new' Front's vote has aptly been defined as less a '*vote de class*' vote than a '*vote de classement*' (i.e., one that expresses social hierarchy rather than a sense of class belonging). See Luc Rouban, 'Le Front national 2002-2017: du vote de classe au vote de classement', *The Conversation*, 8 May 2017.

39   Ipsos/Sopra Steria, '2nd tour présidentielle 2017: comprendre le vote des français', 7 May 2017, ipsos.com.

40   Ibid.

41   Ibid.

than the last'; conversely, Marine Le Pen spoke 'more to the France that is doing less well and those who have the lowest incomes'.[42]

So, it's all right then?

There are at least two arguments to doubt that the defeat of French populism is definitive. Or at least, reasons not to consider that France is completely beyond the shadow cast by the populist challenge. The first reason concerns the size of Macron's victory. While he achieved a clear win in relative terms (his 32 percent advantage over Le Pen was telling) this seems like less of a landslide when we consider the votes received in absolute terms. Out of a total population of 66,990,826 and an electorate of 47,582,183 registered voters, the En Marche! candidate scored 20,743,128 votes: about a third of all French people and 43 per cent of eligible voters. Indeed, the 7 May 2017 second round contest was the presidential election with the highest level of abstention (more than 12 million, 25.4 per cent of the electorate) and the highest number of blank (3,021,499) and invalid (1,064,226) ballots in history. As the Ifop Director of Studies in Politics and Current Affairs François Kraus has observed, this is a 'record level [of abstention] not seen since 1969'.[43] It casts something of a shadow over the winner's true popular legitimation, and above all it reveals the relative decline – a weakening, but certainly not the outright disappearance – of the republican front that had in the past mobilised en masse to defeat the far-Right candidate. In 2002

---

42   Ibid.

43   Cited by Adrien Gaboulard, 'Sondage Ifop-Fiducial: qui a voté Macron et pourquoi?', *Paris Match*, 8 May 2017.

Jacques Chirac beat Le Pen *père* by a margin almost 4.5 million votes greater than the one with which Macron beat Le Pen *fille*, in a clash in which 'we did not see renewed mobilisation driven by an anti-fascist reflex'[44] as was the case with the vote fifteen years before.

In 2002, 3.5 million more people voted in the second round than had turned out in the first, a sign that the contest with Jean-Marie Le Pen mobilised wide sectors of the hitherto 'dormant' electorate. In 2017 there were almost 5 million fewer votes in the second round than the first, a clear symptom of the fact that a significant cohort of Mélenchon, Fillon and Hamon voters stayed at home. And those who did turn out did so with a very low degree of confidence in and identification with the victorious candidate. An interesting analysis of the vote produced by Ipsos/Sopra Steria on the eve of the second round[45] shows that only 16 per cent of those who intended to vote for Macron did so on the basis of agreement with his programme, and just 9 per cent on the basis of his 'personality'. The greater share chose the young new entry, a mysterious object appearing on the French political horizon, on account of the 'political renewal he represents' (33 per cent) or 'out of opposition to Marine Le Pen' (43 per cent), thus handing him a rather generic mandate. This was also unlike the vote for Le Pen, 30 per cent of whose voters said they above all identified with her political programme and only 22 per cent of whom said they were voting out of opposition to the other candidate. This indicated a stronger identification with the substance of her campaign, and indeed a stronger 'party' identification, by a generally less volatile electorate. Also in this case, 41 per cent of Le Pen's voters said that they

44   Ibid.
45   Ipsos/Sopra Steria, '2nd tour présidentielle 2017'.

had chosen her on account of the 'political renewal she represents'. It is telling that in each of these opposed electorates, almost half explained their vote in terms of 'change', that is, a break with the established status quo. For, at root, both the candidates who faced off in the second round embodied some aspect of the populist mood, even if in different, counterposed ways, and only one of them did so explicitly. Fundamentally, however, even Macron, who seemed pro-establishment and pro-Europe, a 'moderate' obedient to the powers that count, was in his own way the bearer of an analogously destabilizing message. He was similarly unwilling to indulge the established parties and political cultures, and like Le Pen called for radical upheaval.

This leads us to the second argument for why we should not be too quick to 'call off the alarm over populism' in France: that is, the nature of Macron's victory (a 'Pyrrhic victory') and the systemic characteristics of the context in which it was achieved and which it is itself bound to condition. The French vote of spring 2017 did not represent a stabilisation of the political system. On the contrary, it revealed and accelerated its collapse (or, we might say, its bankruptcy). This in effect consummated the end of the Fifth Republic: the political order that emerged between 1958 and 1962, held up by the two pillars of the Gaullist centre-right and the Socialist-led centre-left. Between 23 April and 7 May 2017, both of these pillars crumbled. This became fully clear in the first round vote, when the result from the ballot box confirmed that the run-off would be contested between two outsiders. Or better, that the representatives of both the classic Right and Left were now 'outside'. This new reality was well captured by the *Economist*: its report from Paris after 23 April commented, under the subheading 'A New Republic' that 'for the first time in the history of the Fifth Republic, neither mainstream political party has entered the run-off for the presidency.' It explained, 'This first-round result could also presage the break-up of the French party system. It is a measure of the anti-establishment mood that neither Ms Le Pen nor Mr Macron belong to a mainstream, established party'.[46] Particularly dramatic, evident from the very beginning of election night, was the situation of the Socialist Party, which scored a miserable 6.3 per cent, just 2.3 million votes (five years previously François Hollande had taken 10 million at the first round and over 18 million at the second). Here was a political force in the terminal phase of its decline. But the situation of Fillon's Republicans was not so reassuring either: out of the 7 million votes he received in the first round, it was projected that 40 per cent subsequently went to Macron, 30 per cent to Le Pen and the remaining 30 per cent did not vote. Indeed, the impression was precisely that this electorate was becoming fluid and 'leaking out' of the old political containers; that it would never return to its original homes; that French politics would long remain 'liquid', as Zygmunt Bauman would have put it.

There was further confirmation of this in the National Assembly that came out of the parliamentary elections on 18 June: a vote that saw a historic low turnout (42.6 per cent in the second round).[47] This produced the most monochrome

---

46   'Macron and Le Pen advance to the second round of the French election', *The Economist*, 23 April 2017.

47   In total, 18,176,777 out of 47,292,967 registered voters did in fact vote: a 57.36 per cent abstention rate. En Marche! scored 43.19 per cent, followed by the Republicans on 22.23 per cent, the Front National on 8.5 per cent, MoDem on 6.06 per cent, the Socialist Party on 5.68 per cent, La France insoumise on 4.86 per cent, the UDI on 3.04 per cent, the 'miscellaneous Right' on 1.68 per cent, the 'miscellaneous Left' on 1.45 per cent, and the Communist PCF on 1.20 per cent.

parliament in French history, indeed one that was defined as 'Une Assemblée en marche',[48] in which the 'presidential majority' (both Macron's movement and his ally MoDem) elected some 350 MPs. Its yellow colours covered most of the parliament, while the 'PS and the Right registered their worst scores since the beginning of the Fifth Republic [and] La France Insoumise and the FN strengthened their own presence.'[49] This parliament (or, at least, its overflowing *macronniste* centre) was, moreover, packed with *homines novi*, hastily picked in all 577 constituencies in the few weeks following the presidential run-off, following rough criteria that were above all concerned – in paradigmatically populist style – not to give the impression of replicating 'the old'. Most of these figures had no prior political careers: it has been said that 'the 308 MPs arriving in the National Assembly are, for the most part, unknowns who had never belonged to a political party.'[50] Among them we see a particular prevalence of professionals, top managers from both the private and public sectors, university professors and teaching staff, and engineers (reflecting the diverse make-up of 'civil society'.[51] Few of them had

---

48   Louis Hausalter, 'Législatives: voici la nouvelle Assemblée nationale', *Marianne*, 16 June 2017.

49   'The Socialist Party and its allies only got 45 MPs elected [party secretary Jean-Christophe Cambadélis declared the result "an incontrovertible disaster", as he announced his own resignation] while the Right and centre held on to 137 seats. Each of these two political families registered its worst score since the beginning of the Fifth Republic'. Ibid.

50   Adrien Gaboulaud and Anne-Sophie Lechevallier (researchers Chloé Marriault, Apolline Merle, Caroline Petit and Joffrey Pointlane), 'Les députés En Marche! sont-ils tous ni de droite ni de gauche?', *Paris Match*, 23 June 2017.

51   Among the ten categories best represented among En Marche!'s MPs we find in first place 'private sector top managers', then 'Industrialists-Company

administrative experience in public institutions, or had previously held local office (around forty had been mayors, and a few dozen had been local councillors).[52] Only around thirty had already held national office. The level of what Max Weber called 'political professionalism' was, then, very low: and this made this crowd of new 'representatives of the people' particularly dependent on the president and his own persona (for Macron himself was the demiurge from which their 'calling' derived). They will rise or fall with him. Their fate depends on the fortune or misfortune of a leader who looks rather like a monarch. And whose public approval, one year since being sworn in, appears troublingly low – and most importantly, is now in freefall.

Berlin doesn't laugh when Paris is crying . . .

A few months after the French elections, Germany had its own '*trial by fire*'. Here, too, election results had made it look like the 'danger had come to an end'. And here, too, what really happened was that the structure of the political system had (however partially) 'caved in', indeed to the benefit of the 'populist challenger'.

The titles in the German press the following day were telling: 'Despite the losses, the Union was again the winner' (*Frankfurter*

---

heads', 'University professors', 'School principals', then Engineers, Lawyers, Top civil servants, etc. One hundred MPs were 'left-leaning', which is to say that they had or continued to have sympathies for the Socialist cultural milieu (or even participated in some of the Socialist Party's own activities); another forty or so were 'right-leaning' and the rest were 'without known previous allegiances', ibid.

52   'At least 138 LREM [En Marche!] MPs hold or have already held some political office. 42 of them are mayors or former mayors. And 77 of them participate or have participated in a local council', ibid.

Allgemeine),[53] 'Union loses heavily, SPD on record low, AfD third force' (*Die Welt*). On its front page *Die Tageszeitung* published a large picture of the German parliament with a thunderbolt striking it and the caption: 'AfD third-largest faction'. The European press was even more explicit: France's *Le Figaro* headlined 'Bitter victory' (*Amère victoire*) as did Spain's *ABC* ('Amarga victoria de Merkel'). Britain's *The Times* went with 'Merkel win eclipsed by resurgence of far right', and there were similar headlines in *The Guardian* ('Merkel's fourth-term win marred by rise of far right') and *The Financial Times* ('Merkel's fourth-term victory marred by rise of rightwing AfD'). Italy's *La Repubblica* went with 'Hard right and Merkel's losses frighten EU'. These headlines did not show much surprise over an event which surveys in recent months had anticipated. But they did, at least, reflect the impact that this vote had on the political balance in a key European country, and the worries that this had generated.

Moreover, this alarm was more than justified. The numbers indicated, indeed with a certain brutality, that the two parties who had governed together in the previous parliament and who had made up the solid centre of gravity of the German political system over a long period, had suffered un unprecedented haemorrhaging of support. Merkel's CDU/CSU alliance had lost 8.6 per cent vote share compared to the previous elections and Martin Schultz's SPD lost 5.2 per cent, reaching a historic low for his party (20.5 per cent). This loss of support is even clearer if

---

53 'Union trotz verlusten wieder klare sieger', *Frankfurter Allgemeine Zeitung*, 25 September 2017; 'Union verliert stak, SPD auf rekordtief, AfD dritte kraft', *Die Welt*, 25 September 2017; 'AfD Drittestrkste Fraktion', *Die Tageszeitung*, 25 September 2017.

measured in absolute terms: the Christian Democrats and Social Democrats had, all in all, seen the 'migration' of almost 5 million votes since the 2013 contest; this figure climbs to around 8 million when compared to 2005 (the final election before the beginning of the global economic crisis); and reaches as many as 12 million as compared to the last electoral test of the twentieth century, in the 1998 face-off between the two giants Helmut Kohl and Gerhard Schröder. Back then, the two great mass parties represented almost 80 per cent of the German electorate, and they continued to do so for a relatively long time, until the mid-2000s – sometimes governing together in a Grand Coalition, at other times allied with minor parties none too distant from them ideologically and none of which were 'anti-systemic'. Now, conversely, the CDU/CSU and SPD bring together little more than 50 per cent of the electorate, while the other half has been taken over by a growing number of minor parties, one of which – the AfD – is radically anti-establishment, explicitly anti-European and generally anti-systemic in tendency.

It is the 'awkward guest' that has made an imposing rise in the recent period and mixed up Germany's political balances. The sheer size of the AfD vote (almost 6 million, nearly triple its 2013 vote, when it did not surpass the 5 per cent threshold to be represented in parliament) can hardly be ignored. Given its 'ideological distance' from all other political formations, it cannot be included in any governing majority. The speed of its rise means that it constitutes a challenge and a threat to the other parties, which are themselves forced to measure up to its political agenda and the strong points in its propaganda. According to the analysis in vote shifts conducted by Forschungsgruppe Wahlen/ZDF, 21 per cent of the AfD's votes came from the CDU/CSU, 10 per cent from the SPD and 6 per cent from *Die Linke*, while 35 per cent comes from voters who had abstained in previous contests. This confirms German populism's unprecedented capacity to mobilise apathetic and traditionally inactive layers of the German electorate. The territorial distribution of its vote is itself cause for concern: its traditional strongholds are in the former East (it is first-place in Saxony with 27 per cent, and second in all the other eastern *Landern* – Brandenburg, Mecklenburg, Thuringia, Saxony-Anhalt – with percentages around 20 per cent).[54] But it is also conquering new ground in the West, scoring at least 10–11 per cent in Hesse, Rhineland-Palatinate and most importantly Bavaria (where it has torn away a major piece of the electorate from its right-wing competitor, the CSU – sparking a drop of around 8 per cent in this latter's vote).[55]

Warning signs

The AfD's successful result in autumn 2017 was hardly unexpected. The result had been anticipated by a relatively long process that saw the laying of the bases for its rise. The first 'emergency' had in fact been sounded exactly two years

---

54   'The AfD even came in second place in the five large eastern German federal states and eastern Berlin with 21.9 percent of the vote while the Social Democratic Party of Germany (Sozialdemokratische Partei Deutschlands, SPD) fell to fourth place with 13.9 percent of the vote', Christian Franz, Marcel Fratzscher and Alexander S. Kritikos, *German right-wing party AfD finds more support in rural areas with aging populations*, DIW Weekly Report – A policy bulletin from the German Institute for Economic Research, 7–8, 2018, p. 70.

55   These results mark the first time that a right-wing populist party has cleared the 5 per cent threshold for parliamentary representation that has been in effect nationwide since 1953.

previously, in the September of 2016 – that *annus horribilis* of populism in the West – when the symbolically key *Land* of Mecklenburg-West Pomerania went to the polls. Angela Merkel had defined this election a *Schicksalwahl*, a 'fateful vote'; it was also one particularly close to her own heart, in a state she herself represents. The term *Schicksalwahl* highlighted a contest of particular importance: indeed, the reference to 'fate' conjugated with the word 'vote' is a recurrent theme of German political discourse. It was widely used in June 2012 during the Greek general election, when the Germans – alarmed by the words of Alexis Tsipras, who at that time said that 'for us the euro is not a fetish' – made heavy interventions in support of the (corrupt) centrists of New Democracy. They again used it in September 2014 when Scots were asked to vote in a referendum on whether or not they should break from the United Kingdom (and the Germans supported them staying in). And the term returned in June 2016, with the referendum on Brexit.

If the Pomeranian vote was indeed a matter of fate, then fate dealt a real slap to the *Kanzlerin*, fewer than three months after the blow suffered in the British vote. The *Rechtspopulisten* of Alternative für Deutschland (AfD) knocked her own CDU party back into third place by a near two-point margin (20.8 per cent to 19 per cent); it now stood right behind the Social Democratic Party (SPD), still in first place on 30.6 per cent but after having lost over five points.

That spring, other warning signs had come from three other Länder. The fact that these were three such different contexts made them all the more significant as a sample (indeed, one in which almost 15 million Germans headed to the polls). First was the Baden-Württemberg region, one of Europe's biggest economic powerhouses – the *Land* that is home to Mercedes and

Porsche. Here the CDU, which had come first in the previous elections (though a deal between the SPD and the Greens meant that it did not govern) slumped twelve points to 27 per cent and finished behind the *Grünen* (who leapt to 30 per cent). The SPD also lost votes, indeed suffering a genuine debacle, as their vote halved to a paltry 12.5 per cent (together, the two main parties were reduced from 65 per cent of the vote to under 40 per cent). Conversely, the AfD made a triumphant leap from zero to 15 per cent. In Sachsen-Anhalt – unlike Baden-Württemberg, a poor *Land* in the former GDR – the AfD did even better, coming in second place with 24.2 per cent, immediately behind the CDU (which had lost almost 3 per cent) and doubling the score of the SPD, which here, too, collapsed to a score barely above the psychological threshold of ten percent. Only in Rheinland-Pfalz – a middling *Land*, in socio-economic terms – did the SPD hold on, indeed rising slightly; but here, the Greens collapsed (making it impossible to re-run the outgoing SPD–Green coalition). Here, the CDU candidate Julia Klochner failed in her attempt to beat the xenophobes on their own terrain; she had hoped that criticising Merkel's refugee policy would make it possible to take the wind out of the AfD's sails, yet this party ultimately scored an enviable 12.5 per cent . . .

In none of these three *Ländern* would the AfD manage to replicate this regional performance in the 2017 federal vote. But, in Baden-Württemberg, the CDU and SPD lost fifteen percent on their 2013 score, ten percent in the Rhineland-Palatinate and twelve percent in Saxony-Anhalt, whereas in these first and second states the *rechtspopulist* list more than doubled its vote and increased it almost fivefold in the last case.

The AfD: a 'German populism'

Seen in combination, these results offered troubling confirmation of the now endemic – and accelerating – crises of the great 'mass parties' of the twentieth century. In Germany, at least, they seemed to have held on. But this now came to an end, as they faced the emergence of a murky, hybrid, in many senses two-faced party, the fruit of an anomalous grafting together of the different political cultures and 'temperaments' – the worse moods – of its (more plebeian, xenophobic and homophobic) Eastern and (more liberal-conservative) Western sections.

We might say, then, that today the AfD is, as the *Süddeutsche Zeitung*'s authoritative political analyst has written, 'home to an aggressive and crude petty-bourgeois nostalgia', working in the West to gather up the 'feathers of the shattered right wing of the CDU' and in the East to replicate the radicalism and the excesses of the neo-Nazi NPD. Or, as in this same paper put it, the AfD feeds off 'a mix of ethno-regionalism, right-wing radicalism and populism'.[56] It rides on anti-refugee feeling even in the *Länder* in which there are hardly any refugees at all (such as in Pomerania, where there are not even 5,000 of them among a population of 1.7 million – 0.3 per cent of the total!), making a mockery of Frau Merkel's *Wir schaffen das!* ('We can do it!'). During the election, Schwerin, the capital of Mecklenburg, was carpeted in blue AfD posters with 'Stop the migrant chaos' written in block capitals. One of the slogans most often proclaimed by the party is 'Borders closed to migrants, and an end to the euro'. And, every day, it makes fierce attacks on the countries of Southern Europe, in

---

56 Heribert Prantl, 'Das Land darf sich nicht hysterisieren lassen', in *Süddeutsche Zeitung*, 13 March 2016.

particular Greece, accusing them of living off German handouts. Or of being mere sieves, leaking refugees into Europe. Former AfD leader Frauke Petry has sparked controversy with her statements holding that German border guards should be authorised 'to use firearms in case of emergency' to stop refugees entering into the country, as well as her proposal to rename the Migration Ministry the Expulsions Ministry. As was the case during Germany's, and Europe's, darkest days, the AfD advocates expansive demographic policies (another widespread slogan is 'The Fatherland needs children') and uses a rhetoric focused on borders (which should be secure, monitored, exclusionary and closed).

According to an analysis of the 2017 German federal election result carried out by YouTrend, 44 per cent of German voters considered '*Flüchtlinge/Ausländer*' (Refugees/Foreigners) to be the '*wichtigsten probleme*' (main problem), whereas for 24 per cent it was *Rente* (pensions) and for 16 per cent *Soziale Gerechtigkeit* (social justice). This explains the widespread agreement with the AfD's propaganda; for its almost 6 million supporters, the main reason to vote was hostility toward the Chancellor's 'open door' policy (almost 80 per cent of its voters cited this as their motivation, ahead of 'Disappointment over other parties' on 60 per cent). At the same time, the AfD reaped the dividend of its aggressive campaign fought from the 'social Right', radically opposed to neoliberal economic recipes and standing in solidarity with a suffering *Volk* abandoned by Germany's elites. Clearly, it was this combination of an ethnic animus of sometimes explicitly xenophobic undertones with a 'solidarity with the bottom rungs of society' (here, again, the forgotten are identified as the 'left behind' and those sacrificed by liberal cosmopolitanism) that allowed the AfD to conquer the margins of society, the 'gloomy areas' – especially in the former East, but not only there.

An interesting map elaborated by a research group at the European think tank Bruegel shows that the main 'cleavage' of particular significance for AfD support was what it defined as the 'East-West divide'.[57] On a graph in which the vertical axis represents the AfD's vote share and the horizontal one represents the division between East and West, almost all the constituencies in the former East Germany are shown to be located at around 20 per cent, with some scattered as high as 30 or even 35 per cent, while those of the former West Germany are concentrated at the level of 10–12 per cent, with a handful of exceptional cases reaching as high as 15 per cent. Then there are also other cleavages such as the one concerning 'Rural areas' ('districts with lower population density voted more for the AfD than cities and densely populated regions'); age ('districts with a larger percentages of old people tended to vote more for the AfD'); education ('districts with lower education tended to vote more for the AfD, while districts with higher shares of higher education voted less for the AfD') and, naturally, income ('higher disposable household income is associated with lower shares of AfD votes').[58]

---

57   Alexander Roth and Guntram B. Wolff, 'What has driven the votes for Germany's right-wing Alternative für Deutschland?', bruegel.org, 5 October 2017, bruegel.org. See also Martin Stabe and Haluka Maier-Borst, 'German election: AfD's advance in six charts', *The Financial Times*, 20 September 2017, ft.com.

58   Another cleavage was 'Church membership': 'Electoral districts with larger percentages of catholic or protestant church membership voted less for the AfD than electoral districts with higher shares of non-membership in these two churches.' Roth and Wolff, 'What has driven the votes for Germany's right-wing Alternative für Deutschland?'.

There were, without doubt, significant exceptions, like the 'spectacular successes' the AfD obtained in some electoral districts in Baden-Württemberg, 'in particular in the cities of Mannheim and Pforzheim, which were once Social-Democratic strongholds'.[59] This has led many scholars to caution against approaches which assume that the AfD vote is one-dimensional, or those which focus on any one variable. They insist on the need to at least cross-compare the territorial and social-economic factors. This allows us to see that the AfD performed well also 'in Western German electoral districts where there are many employees in the manufacturing industry and where incomes are low'.[60] And that, in fact, the support for established parties decreases, and support for the right-wing populist party AfD rises, in the presence of certain particular traits – over and above the East/West divide – such as a concentration or prevalence of manufacturing industry, and in particular where there are large-scale facilities characterised by 'Fordist' technologies, whose personnel feel threatened by automation and outsourcing. This, indeed, is a psycho-social mechanism very similar to those that exist in the US rust belt and the manufacturing and mining districts of Northern England and of Alsace-Lorraine. In this Germany, too, which has only partly made it out of the twentieth century, the populist wave is fed by a fear (in many cases, becoming an 'anxiety') over being left behind by the new times and supplanted by

---

59 Simon T. Franzmann, 'Alternativa per la Germania: Un partito contro la modernizzazione', *Friedrich-Ebert-Stiftung*, June 2017.

60 DIW Berlin, 'Press Release of 21 February 2018: AfD received more votes in the parliamentary election in rural areas with aging populations', diw.de. 'Support for the AfD increases in districts where there is a high amount of people working in the manufacturing industry as well as in districts where the household income is below the national average', p. 78.

others, and by the frustration and rage of those who feel neglected and unfairly relegated to the margins. Here, too, the prevalent mood is a 'blend of small grievances and historic failures, fears of economic decline and cultural marginalisation, and an overwhelming desire to make the powers in Berlin feel the wrath of the German periphery'.[61]

It may be interesting to compare the profile of the average AfD voter in the autumn 2017 contest with that depicted two years previously, in November 2015, in the Forsa research institute's study for the *Frankfurter Allgemeine Zeitung*. At that time the AfD's followers had been mostly men (72 per cent, up from 68 per cent in 2014), relatively old (72 per cent were over 45); 38 per cent considered themselves 'right-wing' and 45 per cent 'of the centre'. Most importantly, 78 per cent declared themselves 'pessimistic' about the future (23 per cent up on 2014!).[62] As for their family incomes, 28 per cent said that theirs was below €2,000 a month, another 26 per cent between €2,000 and €3,000 and 46 per cent above €3,000. The same study repeated by the same pollster six months later, in May 2016, revealed a further sharpening of this tendency: the proportion of AfD voters belonging to the better-off classes slumped significantly (by 12 per cent) while the poorest (with family incomes under €2,000 a month) rose to 33 per cent. The proportion with relatively higher education levels – *Abitur*, comparable to UK A-levels – fell from 55 per cent to 44 per cent, while those with lower education levels (*Mittlerer Abshluss*, equivalent to UK GCSEs) rose accordingly. The

---

61   Tobias Buck, 'Discontent from Germany's eastern states boosts AfD', *The Financial Times*, 29 September 2017, ft.com.

62   Lisa Nienhaus, 'AfD Ostdeutsch, männlich, pessimistisch', *Frankfurter Allgemeine Zeitung*, 21 November 2015.

percentage openly declaring themselves 'on the Right' rose further (reaching 40 per cent), while those considering themselves 'on the Left') practically disappeared (falling from 17 per cent to 9 per cent). The AfD electorate continued to include large numbers of 'dissatisfied' citizens and those who lacked confidence in any institutional figure, whether that meant the Pope, the Chancellor, or the leaders of the 'official' parties of either government or opposition (the only ones who did draw significant support were the Finance Minister Wolfgang Schäuble and the leader of the Bavarian Christian-Social Union Horst Seehofer, toward whom almost 70 per cent of AfD sympathisers said they had a favourable attitude). The dominant share was those convinced that politicians 'are clueless about everything' and that they, as ordinary citizens, could 'do a far better job'.

Without doubt, the split by the liberal 'professors' led by Lucke in July 2015 had some impact on this shift and on this realignment of the AfD electorate's social base. But, for many of them – very many – the single factor that triggered their choice was the *Wilkommenspolitik* or 'open door' policy and the million refugees arriving in Germany, striking the collective imagination with the force of a military reversal. At the same time, this vote was also driven by a rising feeling of social insecurity, a feeling of existential, social and economic precarity that intensified the traditional German *Angst* – a literary as well as psychological term.

This was the 'accrual of grim, sick, radical angst' which, as the economist Hans Wittgenstein wrote at the time, had hung over the Germans ever since they abandoned their beloved Mark in order to move onto the euro. After all, he explained, for them, giving up the Mark was not like giving up the Lira was for Italians, or the Franc for the French. It was a much more traumatic amputation, in that, for the Germans, the Mark was a substitute homeland, 'Heimat'. It was a place, more than an abstraction: a place in which one is born, to which one returns from journeys abroad. It is the refuge-homestead in which one grows up, where wills are made.[63] This *Angst* now seems to have a stronger basis and more 'material' to feed on – a sense, once again, of deprivation and of social conditions that seem less secure – after the wave of crisis that began in 2009.

A populism for 'rich countries'?

Yet Germany is strong economically. Very strong: it has the highest purchasing power in Europe. It has the fourth highest nominal GDP in the world (after the United States, China and Japan).[64] It is the world's third leading power in terms of imports and exports, with a trade surplus amounting to 8.4 per cent of GDP. It has the highest employment rate (70.9 per cent, 6 points above the European average) and the lowest unemployment rate, at 4.2 per cent[65] (its youth unemployment rate is 7.1 per cent, in contrast to Italy, where

---

63 Hans Wittgenstein, 'Angst nel cuore d'Europa. Sussurri e grida a Berlino', *Apulia*, March 2001. The author, who teaches Economics at Bonn University, wrote that 'Manipulations [like the ones the Italians engaged in with the European tax or the French with the France Télécom pension fund] would not be tolerated by German public opinion, which is possessed by *Angst*: the anxiety that increases as they see their national identity as well as their economic stability being sacrificed.'

64 Germany's nominal GDP amounts to $3,858 billion dollars, and $3,721 at purchasing power parity (PPP), placing it fifth in the world; its GDP per capita is $46,893.

65 June 2016 figures. As the German Statistics Institute Destatis writes in its bulletin, 'The unemployment rate is half the European average, meaning that once again Germany is the European country least affected by the problem of unemployment.'

this figure is close to 40 per cent).[66] Its economy grew by 10 per cent even in the darkest period of the crisis between 2009 and 2014. Its public debt is equivalent to 73 per cent of GDP, a figure which the government plans to reduce to 60 per cent by 2020.

This might suggest that populism in Germany is a 'populism of the rich', and in this sense differs from the 'populism of deprivation' in those countries and societies stained by significant marks of decline, and in which globalisation more openly appears in the form of outsourcing, deindustrialisation and impoverishment. It is almost as if here the populist syndrome – or 'reflex' – assumed the character of a pre-emptive reaction, or fear/foreboding of an external threat coming from an indistinct 'outside' populated by Muslim migrants and free-spending Greeks, Syrian refugees and Italian crooks, all ready to exploit the hard-working, conscientious, ascetic German people, who, for this reason, have to put up new walls in order to defend themselves. This is, then, more a defence of positions that have already been acquired than a reaction to a loss they have suffered. But in reality . . .

In reality, digging even a little under the surface of the data repeated ad infinitum by mainstream news and the system's global agencies, we discover that things are not 'only' like this. That even *Germania felix* has its darker patches and sick parts of its society. Today, Germany is one of the most unequal countries in Europe. While, in 2010, the economy had an overall growth rate of 2 per cent a year, in parallel to this the gap between the richest and poorest layers of society increased (and today there are 12.5 million poor Germans, the highest figure since Reunification). The Gini coefficient – which measures the level of inequality – reached a record high of 0.76 for the distribution of private

---

66   October 2015 Eurostat data.

capital, against a European average of 0.67 (a Gini coefficient of 0 would indicate perfect equality, and 1 a total inequality in which all wealth were concentrated in the hands of a single person). In fact, even this European average has increased over past levels.[67]

This is well-explained in a recent book by Marcel Fratzscher, a professor at Berlin's Humboldt University, Senior Economist at the ECB, and one of the most interesting German economists – indeed, one of the few with a social sensibility. This work has the significant title 'The Fight for Redistribution. Why is Germany Increasingly Unequal?'.[68] It tells us that, despite the myths about Germans' 'high wages', today, real average wages in Germany are lower than they were twenty-five years ago. And while capital income has grown by around 30 per cent since 2000, labour's income has only increased by a feeble 6 per cent in monetary terms. This process has not only deepened the divide between labour and capital, but has split the world of waged labour itself, as higher-waged workers have seen their incomes increase and their lower-waged counterparts see their incomes decrease.[69]

---

67   In Germany the richest 10 per cent of the population holds 63 per cent of overall net wealth. Forty per cent of German families have close to zero net wealth and only 40 per cent are homeowners.

68   Marcel Fratzscher, *Verteilungskampf. Warum Deutschland immer ungleicher wird*, Carl Hanser, Munich 2016. The author is also director of the authoritative economics research institute DIW Berlin (*Deutsches Institut für Wirtschaftsforschung*), and was an adviser to the Merkel government's 2013–17 Economy Minister, the Social Democrat Sigmar Gabriel.

69   In particular, while manufacturing employees are able to resist, for now, with a 4 per cent rise, wages in the services sector are in freefall (–15 per cent) and women still earn 39 per cent less than men for the same work. 'With a Gini coefficient amounting to 0.51, the market wage rate in Germany in 2012 was among the most unequal in all the highly-industrialised countries in the OECD (USA 0.51; UK 0.52; France 0.5; Sweden 0.43).' See

Thus, the 'risk of poverty' has been increasing since 2000, even for sizeable layers of the active workforce. This has generated large numbers of 'working poor' – those who work and count as 'employed' but nonetheless stand on or even below the poverty line. The fact is, not even the data on employment numbers, a strong point of 'German superiority', seem protected from the storm clouds. Of the 43 million 'units' whom the statistics present as 'active' workers, only 7.5 million are in fact employed in the 'second division' labour market, in the most precarious and underpaid jobs classed as 'low-waged work', and, in particular, in the notorious 'mini-jobs' introduced by Gerhard Schröder's SPD government with the so-called Hartz reform in 2003. This introduced a new 'contractual figure', at survival levels designed for short-term periods of work and marginal occupations previously employed cash-in-hand (domestic helpers, babysitters and home carers, newspaper sellers, waiters, etc.). It stipulated a maximum salary of €450 a month for fifteen hours a week's work, at an hourly cost of between five and seven euros and a 30 per cent extra contribution by the employer,[70] amounting to 135 euros, with no holidays, no redundancy arrangements, and almost no provision for pensions.[71]

In reality, many young people's reliance on mini-jobs lasted much longer than the intended brief period in which they first entered the labour market. The mini-job has become an integral feature of the workforce, especially among its female section (70

Alessandro Bramucci, 'Germania sempre piú diseguale', *Sbilanciamoci.info*, 30 December 2016.

70 Two per cent in general taxation and 28 per cent in social security.

71 A study by the German Labour Ministry calculated that the pension contributions resulting from a mini-job will amount to the right to €3.11 a month in pension payments per year worked, and thus a monthly income of €124.40 after forty years worked.

per cent of those on such contracts are women). It was also used for other age categories, including elderly pensioners (numerous over-seventies 'distribute newspapers, stack supermarket shelves and do other unattractive jobs in order to boost their pensions').[72] Over the following decade, the new measure was altered slightly (with a small increase in the maximum pay), but there was an exponential rise in the use of these contracts: numbers more than tripled compared to the first few years, such that it is now estimated that these workers represent around 20 per cent of the labour market (with 4.9 million pure mini-jobbers and 2.7 million *nebenjobbers*, i.e., those who combine a fixed-term or permanent job with a mini-job). And nor are they just employed in the most marginal sectors.[73]

We could add that, in Germany, only a third of thirty- to forty-year-olds have degrees – a percentage lower than the Organisation for Economic Co-operation and Development (OECD) average, and that (in an approach also prevalent in pre-crisis north-eastern Italy) when the government did try to encourage university applications, this provoked resistance from manufacturing businesses concerned by the decline in the number of graduates from the apprenticeship system, which today represents the main channel of the movement from school into work.

---

72 'The group most represented among mini-jobbers according to age group are over-60s, followed by under-25s': Silvia Spattini, 'Le criticità del salario minimo e dei "mini-jobs" in Germania', bollettinoadapt.it. According to the *Süddeutsche Zeitung* 'around 800 000 German pensioners, 120,000 aged over 75 have a minijob'.

73 They are especially concentrated in commercial and artisanal jobs (1,300,000), services (820,000), tourism and the hotels sector (790,000), but also in healthcare (690,000) and even manufacturing industries (596,000). See 'Trabajo precario en Alemania. Los mini-empleos', *Actualidad sociolaboral* (Bulletin of the Spanish Embassy in Berlin), March 2011.

Furthermore, Germany's birthrate is among the lowest in the world, with eight births per thousand inhabitants. This means that, over the next twenty years, over-sixty-fives will reach 24 million in number (a 50 per cent increase) and by 2020 it will be necessary to bring in another million and a half migrants in order to respond to the requirements of production and guarantee the sustainability of the pensions system. And we could also mention that the German banking system is among Europe's most fragile, notwithstanding the vast resources poured into it by government in recent years. There are, then, many fracture lines. Certainly, more than we might imagine, when we just examine the superficial social conditions. Which is not to say that all of them are contributing to the wind in the sails of the AfD.

The 'Third Europe'. Visegrád, and not just there

Perhaps the political scientist Cas Mudde is right. He does not underestimate the size of the AfD's electoral breakthrough, but has questioned the danger it poses for Germany's immediate future, expressing his doubts that it 'is going to be the third force in German politics'. Mudde is perfectly well aware that 'populist radical-right parties can become highly influential' within fragmented party systems 'even if they have "only" 10 per cent or 15 per cent of the vote'.[74] And that, indeed, 'German politics has experienced a "seismic shock".' But he remains convinced that in the AfD's case, its relationship with its electorate is substantially 'weak, and mostly defined by opposition to other parties'. For him, this is apparent in the reasons given for this vote, as

---

74   Cas Mudde, 'What the stunning success of AfD means for Germany and Europe', *The Guardian*, 24 September 2017.

highlighted by pollsters' analysis of voter motivations. Namely, the fact that '89 per cent of AfD voters thought that Merkel's immigration policies ignored the "concerns of the people" (i.e. German citizens); 85 per cent want stronger national borders; and 82 per cent think that 12 years of Merkel is enough'. This would suggest that, rather than being motivated by an articulate political programme, the populist wave has been carried forth (or sparked) by just one, relatively contingent (if powerful) issue, which as such is destined not to have stable effects or ones that will last over time. After all, 'only 34 per cent voted out of conviction for AfD.' For this reason, Mudde argues, 'the current election result mainly shows disalignment from the mainstream parties, rather than re-alignment to AfD.'

These statements are all true and well founded in empirical terms. But there remains the fact that it was the AfD's aggressive, overbearing, publicly visible presence that encouraged and accelerated the electoral slump of the 'system's parties'. And, moreover, the fact that it was the dangerous threat the AfD posed that caused the 'system blockage' that delayed the formation of Germany's government for almost six months (a historic record). Indeed, the AfD provoked the symmetrical lack of openness shown by the potential members of a renewed 'Grosse Koalition' or of an unprecedented 'Jamaica' coalition (Christian Democrats, Greens, Free Democratic Party (FDP)).[75] And lastly, it was the

---

75 The CDU and especially the CSU showed their lack of openness toward the Greens, having decided that they should shift rightward rather than 'leave space' to the populist Right. Similar was the lack of openness shown by the FDP, resistant to allow any further margin of flexibility for the Southern European debtor countries, such as would allow further public bailouts of states and banks, or indeed to accept family reunion for migrants (FDP leader Christian Lindner tellingly stated that it was 'Better not to govern than to

fact that the AfD was 'breathing down the neck' of the SPD – surveys said that it risked overtaking that party – that forced this latter party to abandon the line Martin Schultz announced immediately after the election and to agree to join a fourth Merkel cabinet – a structurally very weak government, destined to usher in an era of troubling instability of a Europe whose German centre of gravity has itself been undermined.

The February 2018 Insa survey, published by *Bild* on the eve of the SPD's own internal referendum on whether to participate in the government, showed that the AfD had become Germany's 'second political force' (at 16 per cent of the vote, ahead of the SPD on 15.5 per cent). All the polls over spring and summer showed the AfD stably above 16 per cent,[76] weakening hopes

---

pretend to govern'). This was symptomatic of the awareness that it was not possible to go on as before, now that there was a 'Eurosceptic force in opposition in the Bundestag, one able to provide a home to that part of the centre-right electorate angered by Merkel's open-border policies and inability to make Eurozone allies respect the rules'. Cfr. Josef Joffe, 'The beginning of the end of Angela Merkel', *Politico*, 22 November 2017, politico.eu.

76 'A survey showed that this week the AfD has overcome the SPD for the first time. According to the opinion poll institute Insa commissioned by *Bild*, the right-wing populist party has improved by one point to 16 percent, while Social Democrats have lost one point and now stand at 15.5 percent' – 'AfD überholt SPD', *Handelsblatt*, 20 February 2018. In a survey by the same pollster in July 2018, the AfD was attributed 16.4 per cent of the vote (with the SPD slightly recovering to 17.3 per cent), while the right-populist party took 17 per cent in the ZDF-Politbarometer in August. The pollster commented 'The AFD achieves its best value so far in the Politbarometer survey', and also noted that 'At the same time, citizens fear that right-wing extremists endanger democracy.' This remark referred to a second dataset which showed that for 76 per cent of those interviewed 'the far Right is a serious threat to democracy.' This sentiment was most of all echoed by SPD voters (91 per cent) and least so by FDP voters (75 per cent), not counting the AfD's own electorate (35 per cent).

that its breakthrough in autumn 2017 had been some mere 'anomaly'. All the more so, given that the populist wave in Germany appears to align troublingly closely with a populist surge shaking up the eastern side of Europe with even more violent force. This is the area that we could call the 'Third Europe', made up of a hard core of ex-Communist countries that were latecomers in the European Union, and to which the eastern constituencies of Germany seem like an impressive appendage. In these countries, *rechtspopulismus* has been a governing force for some time already. They are the four states gathered in the so-called 'Visegrád Group', named after the Hungarian castle-town where in 1335 John I of Bohemia, Karl I of Hungary and Casimir III of Poland held their conference and where in 1991 new leaders created a sort of coordination with a view to their accession to the European Union. The Group consists of Hungary, Poland, Slovakia and the Czech Republic (comprising 64 million inhabitants). Austria, too, has recently joined this populist international.

These are all populisms of a decidedly 'hard' bent, structured around a mix of 'sovereigntyist' nationalism and xenophobia of an identitarian stamp; they are fed by an avowed authoritarian calling, centred on hostility toward the legal system and disregard for civil rights. This has ushered in the explicit theorisation of an 'illiberal democracy' (in which it is still possible to make out the watermark of an old idea bequeathed by the 'people's democracies' of Soviet stamp). Many of their leaders have lived 'other lives' in the Communist nomenklatura, and have transferred their hostility toward human rights and cosmopolitan ideals (as well as 'Europeanism') into the new world, as well as a certain sensibility toward 'material needs' and a communicative approach oriented to their (at least rhetorical) recognition.

Viktor Orbán, the head of the Hungarian government since 2010, is in many ways the ideal-typical representation of this 'new' Eastern European political class. He was a Communist youth leader at high school in the 1980s.[77] At the end of that decade, when Hungary anticipated the fall of the Berlin Wall by liberalising the borders – he was a founder of Fidesz (*Fiatal Demokraták Szövetsége* – 'Alliance of Young Democrats'), born as a radically liberal and democratic youth movement that backed Europe and the free market. He was vice chairman of the Liberal International in 1992, before imposing a sharp right-wing turn on Fidesz the following year. He transformed it from a radical liberal student organization to a centre-right people's party, and from a predominantly urban 'progressive' movement into a conservative party that sank major roots in rural areas (Orbán defined himself 'a village boy').

From then onward, Orbán would be part of the Hungarian political scene without interruption, both as chief of the centre-right government (from 1998 to 2002) and as head of the opposition to the Socialist majority up till 2010, when the powerful wave of protest by 'Hungarians furious with the Budapest elite for the economic collapse' provided fresh fuel for his rhetoric. This encouraged his further metamorphosis into the leading proponent of an aggressively illiberal and nationalist populism 'for the new millennium'. From that point onward, Orbán would increasingly raise the stakes in his battle against the domestic economic and political oligarchy and the (liberal) European establishment. He denounced the migrant-reception policy promoted by Merkel's Germany as 'moral imperialism', rejected the redistribution-by-quota of migrants across Europe, and set up walls and

---

77   He was secretary of the communist youth organization KISZ.

barbed-wire barriers at the borders. He has cut back on civil liberties and the freedom of information and of expression. He has protected some social rights (in terms of pensions, jobs and wages) at the expense of civil and political rights. He has ever more vehemently denounced the 'tyranny of "political correctness" and "mainstream politics" '. In exchange for this, he has secured increasing popular support. In 2010, Fidesz won hands down – an absolute majority (52 per cent), as it scored over 2.7 million votes and crushed the Socialists (the outgoing party of government) who fell from 2.5 million votes in 2006 to less than 1 million. In the 2014 elections Fidesz continued its winning run, despite a small setback (it scored 44.5 per cent of the vote and 133 seats out of 199) before then winning a huge victory in 2018 with a record vote share (2,804,206 votes) in an election in which the second-placed party, with over 1 million votes, was the other far-right party Jobbik (a force just as nationalist, xenophobic and Eurosceptic as Fidesz, and if anything an even more radicalised one).[78] Meanwhile, Orbán's traditional adversary, the Hungarian Socialist Party, practically disappeared from the political scene, falling to a historic low of just 680,000 votes and only twenty seats.

Viktor Orbán is today the true interpreter of the populist challenge coming from the East. His strength also owes to a political and ideological profile that renders him, if not wholly similar to, then certainly compatible with the symmetrical populist wave

---

78   Jobbik has claimed to be 'the only party that "genuinely" stands up for the interests of "the people", and became known for its anti-Roma rhetoric, as well as its clericalism and opposition to European integration', Stijn van Kessel, *Populist Parties in Europe. Agents of Discontent?*, Palgrave Macmillan, London, 2015, p. 50.

coming from the West (from Trump's United States and Brexit Britain). He has thus been aptly portrayed as the politician who

> shapes as much as fits the European zeitgeist': 'His modus operandi is an uncompromising defense of national sovereignty and a transparent distrust of Europe's ruling establishments. He echoes the resentments of what were once called the working and peasant classes, embittered by economic stagnation and resentful of a distant and incestuous political class. He is an economic populist who carves out a strong role for the state, and also a social conservative. He invokes 'Christian values', and makes clear his contempt for the 'corruption, sex and violence' of Western societies. His contempt is for 'liberal elites', the media and greedy bankers.[79]

As he commented in a recent speech to Hungarian diplomats, 'in most European countries – I could honestly say 90 per cent of European countries – there is a gap between the opinion of the people and the policy pursued by the elite.' And we can be sure that the EU's fate, in play in the next European election in spring 2019, will largely be a question of this divide.

Orbán is not alone. Next to him there are others whose political biographies and ideological profile are not much different, for instance, Andrej Babiš, since December 2017 head of government in the Czech Republic. Like Orbán, Babiš has a past in the Communist youth, with important roles both in a large company

---

79 'Viktor Orbán. 'The conservative subversive', in 'The 28 people from 28 countries who are shaping, shaking and stirring Europe: Class of 2016', *Politico*, 2 December 2015.

controlled by the Party (Petrimax) and in the Party itself (it is suspected that he was a 'powerful agent' in the Czechoslovakian secret services (StB) under the code name agent Bureš, and perhaps even a KGB agent). Like Orbán, moreover, he converted to the 'free market', or rather, directly to business itself, upon the fall of the regime, becoming the country's second richest businessman (he has been nicknamed the 'Czech Donald Trump'; other than leading the agro-foods group Agrimax he controls a genuine 'media empire', the Mafra media group). Lastly, like Orbán he created his own party, ANO (founded in 2011; in Czech the acronym, standing for Dissatisfied Citizens' Action, means 'Yes') with the object of 'fight[ing] corruption and other ills in the country's political system'. He rapidly transformed this party into its opposite, namely an instrument of generating support and of covering for his own business affairs, which has itself generated a great number of 'conflicts of interest'.[80] Babiš has often used the party to shield himself from the numerous investigations and charges issuing from the Slovak public prosecutor (earning him the nickname Babisconi, which *Foreign Policy* lumped on him on account of the strong similarity between his political, economic and judicial affairs and those of former Italian Prime Minister Silvio Berlusconi).[81] Despite this, ANO won the October

---

80   As the independent Prague journalist Adam Drda has written 'the Czech Republic is now a paradox: a society disgusted with corruption has given huge power to a man whose business interests amount to the biggest conflict of interest in the country's post-1989 history', Adam Drda, 'Andrej Babiš – Czech oligarch', *Politico*, 25 January 2016.

81   The most serious case concerns the defrauding of the European Union. It regards a €2,000,000 EU subsidy which Babiš allegedly used illegally for his own businesses. He was placed under investigation by the Czech criminal police in December 2015 and then by the European

2017 general election hands down with over 1.5 million votes, triple the score for the second-placed party (the Civic Democratic Party ODC, a free-market, centre-right force that secured 560,000 votes) and over quadruple the score for the social-democratic ČSSD. Winners of the 2013 election with over 1 million votes, the ČSSD now slumped to 355,000! The leader of the largest party in the new parliament, with seventy-eight out of 200 seats, Babiš initially led a minority government (indeed, as the first prime minister from a party other than ODS and ČSSD; he soon also became the 'only incumbent head of government to be charged with a crime by the Czech police and prosecutor'). After losing a vote of confidence (seventy-eight votes for, 122 against), he unexpectedly formed a new government, together with the SPD, and (for the first time since the fall of Communism) was reliant on the external support of the Communist Party, on Eurosceptic and anti-free market positions. This arrangement was based on policies hostile to taking in migrants and aimed at wage workers and the most vulnerable layers of society (that is, to the losers of globalisation).[82]

Things are no better in the other part of the former Czechoslovakia. In Slovakia, which became independent in 1993, the social-democratic head of government Robert Fico, in office

---

anti-fraud office OLAF, for the dual crime of alleged fraud and of wilful damage to the financial interests of the European Union. He was formally charged on 9 October 2017.

82   The second Babiš government's most important 'social' measures include the increase in the minimum wage; the indexing of pensions to the cost of living; the strengthening of the health services; the protection of natural resources from foreign multinationals; an increase in the public sector's role in the provision of essential services; the building of new homes provided at moderate rents; and a roof on housing prices.

since 2016, had to resign in March 2018 on account of a massive scandal concerning the assassination of an independent journalist who had denounced the infiltration of the Calabrian mafia (known as 'Ndrangheta) into his government. Here, national-populist and Eurosceptic parties occupy a major part of the political scene: Fico's party was the largest in the 2016 general election even despite losing almost half its seats (it won forty-nine, against eighty-three in 2012) and had to put together a majority together with the Slovak National Party, an anti-free market, right-wing populist force, and with Most Hid, an ethnically based party representing the Hungarian minority. Both these latter are Eurosceptic.[83]

The party that secured crushing victories at both the presidential and parliamentary elections in Poland in 2015, to the world's horror, is similarly right-wing populist, avowedly national-conservative, and Eurosceptic in tendency. This party, Law and Justice (Prawo i Sprawiedliwość, abbreviated to PiS), was founded in 2001 by the Kaczyński twins, Lech and Jaroslaw. This latter has been the party's monocratic leader since 2010, when Lech died in an airplane crash. Under his leadership, Law and

---

83   The 5 March 2016 elections were a genuine earthquake: Direction – Social Democracy (*Smer – sociálna demokracia*) scored 737,481 votes, 28.3 per cent, a drop of almost 400,000 votes (or 16 percent) compared to the previous elections. Conversely, the Slovak National Party (*Slovenská národná strana*, SNS) doubled its vote (rising from 116,420 to 225,386 and from 4.5 per cent to 8.6 per cent). Meanwhile the neo-Nazi Kotleba – People's Party Our Slovakia (*Kotleba – Ľudová strana Naše Slovensko*) an anti-Roma, anti-migrants, anti-Europe, anti-globalisation and pro-Russian force whose leader Marian Kitleba has his followers call him 'Vodca' (*Duce*) made a breakthrough onto the political stage as it rose from zero to fourteen seats in parliament (over 200,000 votes, 8 per cent).

Justice has taken its candidate Andrzej Duda from an *éminence grise* to the presidency of Poland, with a landslide victory in the 2015 election (5.7 million votes, half a million more than the tally with which Lech Kaczyński became president in 2005) and secured an absolute parliamentary majority with 235 out of 460 seats), placing party Vice President Beata Szydło at the head of the Polish government.

This is the ultimate result of a long process of building hegemony within the Polish political system on the basis of national-populism, after the dissolution of the 'Solidarity Bloc' at the end of the twentieth century. This bloc had been a large centrist space of Catholic inspiration, a directly political extension of the *Solidarność* trade union founded by Lech Walesa. It had managed the confused transition to post-Communism in the 1990s and then broke up into various different fragments. At first, Law and Justice had represented the conservative element of this bloc, but, from 2005 to 2007, it rapidly shifted in a populist direction, rejecting the liberal image that it might have offered at its birth and instead adopting an anti-establishment rhetoric aimed at characterising itself as 'representative of an ordinary, authentic, legitimate "people" against an illegitimate and usurping elite'.[84] Moreover, the party sought to challenge the free-market reforms of the previous political period, with regard to which the popular classes in particular showed

---

84 Stijn van Kessel, *Populist Parties in Europe*, p. 139. As the author writes, 'in the campaign of 2005 "PiS hammered home its new central theme: for well over a decade liberal reforms had wreaked havoc on the fortunes of ordinary folk". All in all, apart from its already prevalent anti-establishment discourse, marked by the aim of fighting corruption and pushing for further decommunisation and lustration, PiS strengthened its rhetorical appeal to the "ordinary people" and, thus, became a more unmistakable populist party', ibid.

increasing hostility and disillusionment. At the same time, the party became more explicitly Eurosceptic and emphasised its 'solidaristic' character. This allowed it to intercept and absorb a large part of the electorate of the other two populist parties: Self Defence (SO) and the League of Polish Families (LPR). Law and Justice is not populist only in terms of its style and rhetoric, but also its electorate, which is very similar to that of the other 'new populisms' we have considered. Its main strong points are among working-class constituencies and union members, as well as among miners, shopkeepers, farmers, the unemployed and pensioners. In this case, too, PiS is strong in rural and peripheral areas and weaker in the big cities. It provides further confirmation of the fact that if we want to 'read' the populist phenomenon in the new millennium, maps are more eloquent than tables of statistics: not only the socio-economic map, but also the historical one. As we already saw in the American and British cases, the *longue durée* dynamics tend to re-emerge over the ruins of the political cultures of the twentieth century, revealing older dividing lines. Revealing, in the Polish case, is one such dividing line that dates back to the period immediately subsequent to the Congress of Vienna in 1815 and the territorial partition of Poland among the Empires. It is telling that even in the 2007 contest – and this was noted at the time – the Kaczyński brothers' vote was higher to the east of the 17th meridian, in the old Galicia and Lodomeria, in what was Congress Poland, subaltern to Tsarist Russia, and in the Grand Duchy of Krakow, annexed to the Habsburg Empire. Faced with an electoral map almost exactly divided in two, with an entirely orange Western area (the colour of the districts where the moderate conservatives and liberals of Civic Platform, PO, had emerged victorious) and a uniformly blue eastern area (representing Law and Justice), one sharp online maps commentator observed that 'this isn't just some urban/ rural, professional/worker, white-wine-and-brie/beer-and-sausages thing!' but a rather more historically determined one. For 'the divide between the (more free-market) PO and the (more populist) PiS almost exactly follows the old border between Imperial Germany and Imperial Russia, as it ran through Poland! How about that for a long-lasting cultural heritage?!?'[85]

In 2015, this same political and territorial division was reaffirmed in even sharper definition: Law and Order swept home in all the districts in former Congress Poland, winning sometimes large majorities of the vote (in Lublin it took ten seats as against three for PO; in Chelm it won by eight to two, and in Rzeszów by twelve to two) and in the former Grand Duchy further to the south (by eight to one in Nowy Sacz and seven to two in Krosno), just above the border with Slovakia. But it was weaker in the western part of the country, where seat numbers were close to a draw; in some major urban centres like Poznán it was the PO that prevailed.

To complete this 'historical' map, we are missing only Austria. And, at the end of 2017, it did indeed make itself felt. The black wave of populism-in-government on the Eastern European front now touched the far southern border of the old Habsburg Empire, with the formation of an executive with a strong conservative-populist bent, after the election won by Sebastian Kurz (Federal Chancellor) and Heinz-Christian Strache (his Vice Chancellor). And it was an especially resounding victory for this latter, the

---

85 The comment by a certain David G.D. Hecht is cited by Frank Jacobs, a blogger and specialist in strange maps (indeed, this is the title of his blog) in his article 'Polish Election Map Reveals Old Imperial Border', bigthink.com.

leader of the *Freiheitliche Partei Österreichs* (FPÖ). Strache has been the protagonist of an extraordinary recovery which has seen the FPÖ rise from the 490,000 votes it achieved 2002 (after its collapse under previous leader Jörg Haider) to its current share of 1,316,000 votes, a historic high. This owes to a campaign that hammers away at anti-immigrant and anti-Muslim themes, wrapped up with a strong anti-establishment polemic and a sharp nationalist rhetoric. *Heimat im Herzen* (Homeland in the heart) and *Arbeit statt Zuwanderung* (Jobs instead of immigration) are among its favourite slogans, which do not differ greatly from those of the new and aggressive leader of the Austrian People's Party (ÖVP), Sebastian Kurz, who after securing 98 per cent backing to become ÖVP leader in May 2017 imposed a strong conservative and generally populist shift on this traditionally centrist formation, which had until then been allied with the SPD in government. It was Kurz, moreover, who as Interior Minister threatened to build a barrier at the Brenner Pass to seal off the border with Italy and stop the migrant 'invasion'.

And beyond that border, immediately to the south, Italy now awaited its own turn.

6

Italy's 'Three Populisms'

March fool

'For fuck's sake!', exclaimed the Luxembourg foreign minister Jean Asselborn, in a televised row with Italian Interior Minister Matteo Salvini on 14 September 2018. Both men were taking part in the Conference on Migrants and Security in Vienna, organised by the Austrian presidency of the EU. This was an unprecedented incident at any international summit; it was indicative of the trauma that Italy's change of government has produced around Europe.

The general election of 4 March 2018 represented a genuine earthquake, the effects of which were not only felt within Italian borders. It saw the victory of two self-proclaimed anti-establishment forces, both of which are Eurosceptic in tendency – the Five Star Movement (M5S) and Lega Nord. This in turn opened the way to the constitution of a 'yellow-green' (representing the parties' respective colours) government that bounced the country into the so-called 'populist' camp. It has created threatening cracks in Europe's political balance. Indeed, in early 2018, the 'black knight of global populism' Steve Bannon chose the centuries-old Certosa di Trisulti, central Italy, as home for his own 'leadership school'. Restoring the *Roman caput mundi* of the days of Empire, Bannon enthused that Rome is 'at the centre of the political universe' and described what is taking place there as 'extraordinary'. He saw in the Italian vote the sign of an epochal turning point: 'you have struck a blow at the heart of the European beast, of foreign capital, of the foreign opposition media.'[1]

Once again, the maps portray the true character and dimensions of this phenomenon better than do tables of statistics. The language of colours speaks louder than the language of numbers, here: the two-coloured map that resulted from the 4 March election speaks for itself, with the South almost uniformly in yellow (M5S's colour) and the North almost all in a blueish but ever greener hue (as the colours of the centre-right alliance change from Forza Italia blue to Lega green). Here were two Italys; up top, the one that we might say belongs to 'Visegrád', having brought across the Austrian corridor the spirit of Hungary, Poland, the Czech Republic and Slovakia: the insensitive fury of the stingiest partners of a Europe which has itself become ever meaner. Below that is the old Italy of Masaniello (in 1647 a rebel leader in Naples, in an uprising against the Spanish regime), an Italy immersed in its Mediterranean desperation, its abandonment, after the old networks of mediation through local notables have been blown up by the lack of liquidity. Here, the demand for help has, in a sense, become terminal. And, between this yellow and green, there is very little, almost nothing: just the scarlet spot in the former 'red regions', now eroded and reduced to a mere

---

1   Luca Romano, Bannon e il governo M5s-Lega 'Un colpo per la bestia Europa', *Il Giornale*, 3 June 2018.

residue after Renzi's catastrophic experiment. This pattern becomes even clearer and more explicit if we look not at the coalitions but the individual parties which came first in each respective electoral college or province: here, the Five Star yellow covers the whole South and Lega green the whole North, with the red strip in between even thinner and smaller.

The Italian political system of the so-called 'Second Republic' – born in the mid-90s with the rise of Silvio Berlusconi and then consolidating as the duopoly of centre-right and centre-left – no longer exists. Its two pillars – Forza Italia and the Democratic Party (PD) – have been eroded and marginalised. Their electoral strength and political power have been hollowed out by the 'biblical exodus' of their respective voters. This latest structural metamorphosis in the Italian political system has been registered in a study by the analysts of LUISS university's Electoral Studies Centre CISE.[2] They speak of an outright 'apocalypse in the moderate vote',[3] which has seen 18 million voters leave its ranks in just ten years. The researchers calculate that, between 2008 and 2018, the PD and PdL (the sometime name of Berlusconi's Forza Italia vehicle) lost around 16 million votes (7 million for the former, 9 million for the latter) and that another couple of million evaporated with the disappearance of the residual forces of the 'centre'. As the authors summarise, 'The mainstream parties – those political forces that make up part of the People's, Socialist and Liberal Democratic groups in the European parliament (EPP, PES, ALDE) – counted for just over 30 million votes in 2008, around 83 per cent of all valid votes, whereas now they have

---

2   Vittorio Emanuele, 'L'Apocalisse del voto moderato: in dieci anni persi 18 milioni di voti', CISE, 12 March 2081, cise.luiss.it.
3   Ibid.

been reduced to just 12.3 million.' They add that, at the same time, the Lega (no longer only the 'Northern' League, after Salvini assumed the leadership and made it a nationwide force) 'quadrupled its own support'. And that 'the strategy of Renzi's PD, which aimed at conquering the centre ground and hinged its approach on Europe and civil rights measures, led to the worst result for the Left in the history of the Republic.'

Thanks to analysis of the shifts in the vote we also know approximately where these 18 million political nomadic voters went over the course of that decade: 60 per cent fed the wave of support behind the Five Star Movement, making it *the* event of the last ten years; 20 per cent 'swelled the ranks of the radical (or "sovereigntist") Right', most importantly 'new Lega'; while the remaining 20 per cent went to abstention. 'This allows us to understand', CISE concludes, 'that this is not only a matter of volatility'; rather 'the system has literally been turned upside down.'[4] 'The moderate, pro-European, mainstream centre of gravity has been blown up' both because the PD's haemorrhaging of over half of its vote has fed the droves of support behind the Five Star Movement and because the emptying-out of Forza Italia has swollen the ranks of the Lega, overturning the balance between moderate and radical forces within the centre-Right ('in 2008 the balance was 3.5 to 1 in favour of the [moderate Right], whereas now it is 1.5 to 1 in favour of the [radical Right]'). Looking at the wider political balance, the researchers conclude that, while ten years ago, pro-system forces had a 5.5 to 1 advantage (30 million to 5.5 million votes), today the opposite is the case: there are 20 million anti-establishment voters against barely 12 million for the establishment (a proportion of 1 to 0.6).

---

4   Ibid.

In the Italian political laboratory

Italy's 'populist explosion' ought not be a surprise. Its roots lie in a medium- to long-term dynamic that has made Italy the holder of at least two undesirable 'records', which make it a case study of sorts. What is now called 'neo-populism' had already come early – *avant la lettre*, we might say – already in the last decade of the twentieth century. Italy was remarkable because of the multiple forms it took in this country. But also because of the ultimate outcome: the establishment of a 'twice-populist' government in one of the countries that has participated in the European project from the outset. In fact, in Italy, populism appeared not in one variant but three, which followed one after the other in (relatively quick) succession. We could call these three 'forms' and three 'figures' of neo-populism by the names of their eponymous 'heroes': Berlusconism, Grillism and Renzism. The three differ in terms of the timing of their 'rise' and their 'period of hegemony', as well as in terms of their 'political culture' – if such a weighty term can be applied to such phenomena. But they are also united by certain traits they have in common, and not only at a formal level.

All three of these political experiences are characterised by a strong *personalisation*. As we can see from the names attached to them, they are each inseparable from the person who, so to speak, 'invented' and 'interpreted' them (in the sense of an actor in a play) on the stage of national politics. Moreover, all three deployed some kind of 'disintermediation mechanism' (even if they differed in type); that is, a style of communication and of action, based on a direct relationship with a generally indeterminate audience that stretches beyond the traditionally settled terrain that had been politically and culturally delimited by the political forces that went before. Something that could look like 'the people', if for no other reason than because it is targeted with a popular (or perhaps, 'pop', as in 'pop music) style of communications. Lastly, all three of these protagonists tend to present themselves, and their own respective movements, parties or factions, in terms of a *rupture* – differentness, a new beginning. They present themselves in terms of their distance, or rather, their claimed distance, from a past or a present that are written off as a mere accumulation of ills, at the same time as they use hyperbole or make 'unrealisable promises'.

Without doubt, all three of these 'political styles' have assumed the identifiable characteristics of the 'new populism', such as it has been interpreted (and defined) in the public debate by columnists and TV pundits. Following Diego Ceccobelli's distinction of this media definition of populism and more 'scholarly' definitions, the populism as it is presented by 'mass media' discourse is 'pop politics', 'demagogy' and 'novelty'.[5] But, as an informal survey of these phenomena shows, the conception of populism that has emerged in the 'scholarly debate' also applies to each of these cases, even if they also exhibit certain rough edges.[6]

---

5 Diego Ceccobelli, 'Che cos'è il populismo', valigiablu.it, 30 December 2016, valigiablu.it.

6 Ceccobelli here refers to Cas Mudde's well-known definition. He distils it afresh in a formula which considers populist only those forces that 'elaborate a programme and messages in which the people, seen as a single indivisible unit (thus rejecting the concept of pluralism) and as the bearer of positive values, is set in opposition to (political, economic, financial, etc.) elites considered corrupt (it thus counterposes itself to elitism, the opposite of populism)', ibid.

Berlusconian 'tele-populism'

When Silvio Berlusconi won the Italian general election in March 1994, he appeared as a black sheep – both in his own country and at international summits. Bill Clinton had not long beforehand been elected in the United States, on a landslide for the Democrats. In the United Kingdom, the Conservative John Major, who had succeeded Margaret Thatcher, had swept home at the 1992 general election, defeating the Labour competition by almost 10 per cent; the Scottish National Party was still on just 1.9 per cent and won only three seats. The only crack in Britain's two-party system were the Liberal Democrats, who are anything but populists. In France, the Socialist President Mitterrand was reaching the end of his second term (after a big win over his immediate opponent Chirac in the previous election), while Jean-Marie Le Pen was still ghettoised. Lastly, in Germany, Helmut Kohl ruled unopposed, rich on the 41 per cent scored by his own CDU and its Bavarian CSU ally, while the SPD followed on 36 per cent (thus together making up almost four-fifths of the German electorate). Berlusconi was literally an 'unidentified object'.

The 16,585,516 votes counted on the night of 28 March 1994 – 43 per cent of the total – truly represented a thunderbolt in a clear blue sky. No one had predicted this, even two months previously: no survey, no analyst, no observer, no media, had seen it coming. Nor could anyone have imagined that he could win as many as 3,277,272 more votes than the so-called 'joyous war machine' deployed by Achille Ochetto (leader of the Democrats of the Left, heir to the Communist Party dissolved in 1991), sustained and fed by the thousands of tried-and-tested activists and 'professional politicians' at the head of the powerful Alliance of

Progressives. Nor was it easy to understand exactly whence these votes had come: from what political culture, from what social subject, from what layer of Italian society. The political creature that Berlusconi had brought together behind the scenes, almost as if in a laboratory – then as now, one would struggle to call Forza Italia a 'party' – had all the characteristics that political scientists attribute to the 'instant party'; that is, a party 'born from nothing at the will of skilful leaders who cohered a heterogeneous set of forces around themselves, transforming them into a mass base'.[7] Berlusconi himself was a total outsider. He was an absolute beginner in politics: a billionaire businessman who had never even worked an hour in public administration, who had never joined a party (at most joining the ranks of P2, an illegal masonic lodge involved in criminal activities). He had been a sympathiser of Prime Minister Bettino Craxi (eventually convicted of far-reaching corruption) for self-interested reasons, rather than out of any concern for Craxi's PSI party.

Berlusconi brought together – indeed, very early on – two of the typical characteristics that would later be attributed to the 'new populism', at least formally speaking: total personalisation, and absolute novelty. His Forza Italia had nothing of the traditional party – the model on which all the parties of Italy's so-called First Republic, from the Communists (PCI) to the Christian Democrats (DC) and the neo-fascist Italian Social Movement (MSI), had been based. As was written at the time, Forza Italia

---

7 Doriano Pela, 'L'identità politica tra pubblico e privato', in Paolo Sorcinelli and Daniela Calanca, eds., *Identikit del Novecento: conflitti, trasformazioni sociali, stili di vita*, Donzelli, Rome, 2004, p. 266.

has no precise ideological matrix, nor a cultural inheritance other than a generically Catholic and liberal inspiration. It has no political story behind it: conceived as an advertising campaign, a media-political marketing operation, it sprung up in just a few months, in a blitz effect.[8]

Almost all the MPs elected on its lists (and there were a lot of them) were either managers from Publitalia – Berlusconi's advertising agency, which operated as its organisational hub during the electoral campaign – or lawyers, professionals and entrepreneurs linked to his company's business dealings.

Such was Forza Italia's 'formal' aspect. But Berlusconism corresponds to a neo-populist matrix also in terms of its substance and the content that is conveyed by its rhetoric. We need only look at Berlusconi's famous 'message to Italians' in 1993, with which he announced his decision to 'enter the fray' (and he used the word *scendere*, 'descend', as if coming down from the heights of Olympus). As he said (and then wrote, and then broadcast everywhere he could):

Italy is the country that I love. It is here that I have my roots, my hopes, my horizons. It is here that I learned my calling as an entrepreneur, from my father and from life itself. And here I also learned the passion for freedom. I have chosen to enter the fray and to concern myself with public affairs, for I do not want to live in an illiberal country governed by immature forces and men intertwined with a politically and economically bankrupt past.[9]

---

8   Giovanni Valentini, *La Repubblica*, ibid.

9   Silvio Berlusconi, Videomessaggio agli italiani, 26 January 2004, YouTube video, <youtube.com/watch?v=3OlQ762Qh-A>.

Here were all the ingredients of classical populism: 'popular' (we could say, 'pop') language. It gave the image of a man who came from the outside, from society – from its higher echelons, but still from a sphere other than politics, from the 'trench of work' – and who learned his own calling from his family and 'from life itself'. The image of the chasm between the degradation Berlusconi identified as left behind by others – by those 'up above', in the Palaces of Power – and the future marvels he could promise to those in the offices, the warehouses and in the street. And here, too, was the tone of 'emergency' that had forced his choice – presented as a new Cincinnatus, compelled to enter public affairs in order to avert the public ruin.

This was, then, a matrix that had already been tried and tested. But, in Berlusconi's political experience, there was also a new feature which cannot be reduced to any of the past forms of populism. This was well-grasped by one attentive and studious observer, Pierre-André Taguieff,[10] who coined the new term 'tele-populism' in order to define this phenomenon. A populism 'changed by technology', we could say. And one redeveloped thanks to its encounter with a particular medium – television – that changes the relationship between leader and people. And it works on the institutional matrix itself, 'turning' the traditional representative democracy into a 'video-politics'. This was Giovanni Sartori's insight in his work introducing the figure of the *Homo videns* and the metamorphosis of power into 'Video-Power'.[11]

---

10 Pierre-André Taguieff, *L'illusion populiste*, Berg International, Paris, 2002.

11 Giovanni Sartori, *Homo videns, Televisione e post-pensiero*, Laterza, Rome-Bari, 1999; Giovanni Sartori, 'Video-Power', *Government and Opposition*, 24(1) spring 1989, pp. 39–53.

The 'new demagogue' highlighted by Taguieff is above all a snake-oil salesman, who, in 'celebrating his own differentness', or 'uniqueness', addresses himself to the people 'to make it dream: he is the man of all promises, who ideally seeks to reach all types of audience',[12] as only TV can do. He is thus a 'telegenic demagogue', a 'great actor of the era of video politics', like – in their own different ways – Ross Perot in the United States, Bernard Tapie in France, and of course Berlusconi in Italy. But Berlusconi is not just better than the others at using TV; he *is* TV. He is the near-monopolist owner of the TV stations. And as such, he is the inventor of a 'televisual genre'. His deeper message is broadcast not only via those segments of the palimpsest of overlapping news reports and political debate (though it also advances along these avenues, indeed pervasively so). It also proceeds by way of entertainment shows, soaps, even adverts – by means of the styles they broadcast, in the anthropology that they build up, in the repertoire of values that they break apart and in the new ones they replace it with.[13] When Berlusconi railed against 'political theatre', he did so in order to replace the obsolete live audience with the infinitely more powerful one carried by the magic of the small screen, reinventing the world at his own whim in every dining room in Italy.

In this sense, Taguieff suggests that, in the era of his initial rise and success, Berlusconi was a perfect 'tele-cultural' hero – to use

---

12 Taguieff, *L'illusion populiste*, p. 121.

13 See, on this, Norberto Bobbio (with Giancarlo Bosetti and Gianni Vattimo), *La sinistra nell'era del karaoke*, edited by Francesco Erbani, Reset, Milan, 1994, p. 36.

the category coined by Marc Augé[14] – who was able to sell the 'strategy of seduction and subversion (more than of succession)'[15] in a typical 'situation of *surmodernité*' characterised by a triple surplus: the 'excess of events, linked to the influence of the media; the excess of images, subject to the same influence; and an excess of individualisation, linked to the ditching of collective cosmologies'.[16] That is, he made his breakthrough in the particular context of the first spasms of the globalisation that would shape subsequent decades with a disruptive force equivalent to the effects of a war. This was, still, a soft and friendly globalisation. It encouraged the emergence of a populism of 'easier times', over the ruins of the old order: a populism that corresponded to a hedonism born of an impetuous and grasping sense of well-being based on *carpe diem*.

Lastly, there is a final characteristic of Berlusconian populism well captured by Roberto Biorcio in his well-researched volume on 'Populism in Italian Politics': namely, 'the promise of immediacy, the rejection of the complexity of the decision-making processes set out in the Constitution';[17] or, as Giovanni Orsina has observed 'the speed and efficiency of the new class of non-professional politicians, and their leaders in particular'.[18] This was Berlusconian populism's very particular way of working its way into Italy's tormented transition, at a moment in which the

---

14   Marc Augé, *A Sense for the Other*, Stanford University Press, Stanford, 1998.

15   Taguieff, *L'illusion populiste*, p. 123.

16   Augé, *A Sense for the Other*, pp. 128–9.

17   Roberto Biorcio, *Il populismo nella politica italiana. Da Bossi a Berlusconi, da Grillo a Renzi*, Mimesis, Milan, 2015, p. 72.

18   Giovanni Orsina, *Il berlusconismo nella storia d'Italia*, Marsilio, Padua, 2013, p. 171.

country was experiencing a fundamental transformation of its political system. Its rise came right after Tangentopoli, the series of trials in which the courts' work cleared out the whole existing political-parliamentary landscape. None of the previous parties' names survived into the new political era (with the exception of flotsam and jetsam like the Republicans and the Radicals): from the Communist PCI to the neo-fascist MSI via the Christian Democracy, the parties either disappeared entirely, changed their name and their skin, or simply started imitating something else.

Berlusconi's instant party gave shape to this void – as, indeed, have all of the post-twentieth-century neo-populisms. Around the shell of the 'party-business' he gathered a heterogeneous constellation that brought old forms of conformism together with new forms of revolt, and the reactionary conservatism of the old silent majority with the post-Marinettian futurism of modernisers without principle. But only in part were these forces gathered *within* this shell. Berlusconi's success also owed to a bold operation in electoral engineering, as he federated all the previously existing populisms together, in a logic which varied depending on the local geography. Hence, in Northern Italy, Berlusconism allied with the ethnopopulism of Umberto Bossi's Lega Nord, and in the South, he allied with the post-fascist and late-*qualunquista* populism of Gianfranco Fini. This guaranteed his coalition a heterogeneous but relatively stable base of support.

Seen in this light, the fact that neo-populism arrived in Italy earlier than anywhere else is rather less surprising. Fundamentally, the Italy of the early 1990s only anticipated – driven by the disruptive force of the 'moral question', or better, of the 'judicial question' – the latent systemic crisis that would take over the whole mature West fifteen years later, under the impulse of a fully developed globalisation.

Grillo's 'cyber-populism'

From the point that Berlusconi first announced that he was entering the fray, exactly two decades would pass – the time it took for this cycle to run out of road – before we would see the emergence of the second type of Italian neo-populism, in February 2013. Again, it came almost 'without any warning', in national terms at least – and to a degree no one had predicted. This was the moment of the Five Star Movement's electoral breakthrough, as it became the country's single most popular party. While everyone, or almost everyone, had expected at least a narrow victory for Pierluigi Bersani's Democratic Party, Beppe Grillo burst into the spotlight with his 8,689,168 votes (45,000 more than the Democrats). While the Democrats made off with the seat bonus for the largest coalition (thanks to their soon-dissolved arrangement with the centre-left SEL), it was Grillo's party that had taken centre stage. The Democrats achieved only a 'mutilated victory'[19] that would characterise the whole subsequent parliamentary term.

It is worth emphasising that this was no repeat of 1994. This time, we did not have a new political entity materialising 'out of nothing', as was the case with Berlusconi two decades before. This was not a second 'instant party'. Rather, what we saw was the explosion, at the very heart of the institutional system, of a

---

19   As Italians called their disappointment at the Versailles Treaty after World War I, which did not reward them their territorial claims despite the sacrifices made and the fact they were on the winning side.

movement that had long been growing in the 'belly' of Italian society. This was the emergence on the institutional terrain of a movement that had hitherto remained under the surface. Almost six years had passed since the first 'V-Day' on 8 September 2007, when a 'movement' formed online made its 'physical' debut on city squares around Italy. We have to go back even further into the millenium to the first moral and civic battles that had been fought, even before the official founding of the Five Star Movement: 'Clean Up Parliament' (2005), 'Out of Iraq' (after the death of Nicola Calipari), 'Tango Bond' (again in 2005, in a battle against the banks that had drugged their own customers on Argentinian Treasury bonds), 'Research Gagged', 'ShareAction Let's Take Back Telecoms', as well as battles against incinerators, against pointless big public works projects and against the state financing of newspapers. And then came the local electoral victories, from mayor Pizzarotti in Parma to its resounding victory in the Sicilian regional contest. But the *sorpasso* ['overtaking'] of the PD at the 2013 general election doubtless marked a turning point. Indeed, an unforeseen one.

It came after a new and equally sharp break in the Italian political system. That is, after the fall of the last Berlusconi government, which also marked the end of his own long political cycle: an extra-parliamentary crisis produced by the 'spread' (i.e. the difference between Italian and German bond yields) reaching 750 points (equivalent to an Italian default). This crisis was governed from above (and, in part, from outside forces). But, most importantly, it came after more than a year of political apnoea, in which all the parties disappeared from the scene, shielded by a government of technocrats. Having delegated full power to this cabinet, they also gave their almost unanimous agreement for its policies, which produced a social bloodbath. We could call this a sort of 'long night of politics' (if for no other reason than that Italy's political forces and their representatives had ended up 'in the dark', standing in the wings as the men and women of Mario Monti's cabinet did their work). When this night came to an end and the Italian political system re-emerged into the light, it appeared in a structurally altered form: now it was no longer bipolar – or at least bipolar in tendency, as in recent years, with the centre-Left and the centre-Right – but tripolar. Between these two now-reduced poles emerged a third one, a source of trouble whose very presence radically changed the political landscape.

In this 'epiphany', 'Grillo's movement' (and at this point M5S still was *his* movement) revealed itself as an explosive, transversal force, rather like all the contemporary neo-populist phenomena (i.e. the ones following the 2009–10 crisis). It worked as a 'spirit level' as it harvested support in all sectors and all areas of Italy's social, generational, territorial and political malaise. This is well accounted in the 'photograph' of Italy taken in the immediate aftermath of the vote by Tito Boeri and Tommasso Nannicini (a pair who know how to handle data) based on the figures for 8,013 *comuni* (municipal areas).[20] They looked at what they termed the 'new electoral geography', and found that what defined itself as a 'non-party' everywhere swept to victory – in big *comuni* as in small ones, in rich ones as in poor ones, in the North as in the South, with percentages ranging between 20 per cent and 30 per cent in the very large majority of cases. Its advance was relatively indifferent to the Left–Right divide – and, in general, the articulation of traditional political cultures – and, instead, followed a sort of 'hydraulic' logic, an apparently 'natural' phenomenon

---

20   Tito Boeri and Tommaso Nannicini, 'Come il voto ha cambiato i partiti', *la voce*, 12 March 2013.

(that is, more like a shift in 'nature' than in politics, in the manner of a tsunami or a seismic shock). It drained from the centre-Right's reservoir of votes as from the centre-Left, in proportion to the specific territorial weight of each of these two sides: it took more votes from the centre-Right in the South, where that had been the stronger pole, and more from the centre-Left in the North.[21] It gathered more than 40 per cent support among both dependent and independent workers and monopolised the youth vote. The PD retained its lead only among pensioners, and Berlusconi's PdL only among housewives: the two categories that spend most time in front of the TV. And this, too, is a 'sensitive' matter.

In fact, the decline of TV – the most generalist medium, and one that has dominated the world of communication for over half a century – as an instrument for organising consensus and orienting preferences (including electoral ones) has been identified as one of the causes of the parallel decline of Berlusconism and its particular populism (appealing to TV viewers) has dissipated or in any case thinned out a great deal). And the emergence of the web as a new, all-encompassing media universe can itself be identified as a defining factor in the parallel emergence of *grillismo* and its innovative 'cyber-populism': the form of expression and organisation of the emerging 'people of the web', or, as its eponymous hero calls it, 'the people of the Net'. We could even say, then, that each new communications technology has its own form of populism.

And that is doubtless true. The use of 'networks' and the 'rhetoric of the Net' – this latter was referred to a revolutionising

---

21   See my *Dentro e contro. Quando il populismo è di governo*, Laterza, Rome-Bari, 2015, p. 16.

factor able to reshape the foundations of politics and the practice of democracy (i.e. the technical possibility of a direct, instant democracy in which we can participate remotely, a fundamental and in some regards fundamentalist democracy) – were theorised to exhaustion by the Grillo–Casaleggio duo.[22] The Internet was the technological basis for organising the meetups and the various V-Day mobilisations and more locally centred flashmobs. But the full picture is also rather more complex. As Carlo Freccero – perhaps Italy's leading expert on the world of communications, and certainly the most talented[23] – has convincingly shown, Grillo was not only (we could even say, 'not so much') the political entrepreneur who first invested in the web (though even this would be quite something, in the era in which all the others were still wrangling to secure themselves a slot on some TV talk show). More importantly, it was Grillo who was first able to combine to great effect *all* the available media – the new ones but also the old and even the very oldest. He produced a sort of media hub; he ran his own blog, but also played his own role as a former TV comedian (one who remained impressed on the collective visual memory); he snubbed the TV cameras, but also ended up on all the news shows because of his verbal successes, if only thanks to the fact that he was attacked by the presenters and his political competitors; he remained in virtual form in cyberspace, but could also fill the city squares with bodies, in the oldest means of political socialisation of all (think of the conclusion of the electoral

---

22   Gianroberto Casaleggio and Beppe Grillo, *Siamo in guerra. Per una nuova politica*, Chiarelettere, Milan 2011.

23   'Grillo, la tv e il cinema di Matarazzo. Intervista con Carlo Freccero', *Europa*, 23 February 2013; Carlo Freccero, *Televisione*, Bollati Boringhieri, Turin, 2013.

campaign in Rome's Piazza San Giovanni on 22 February 2013). He could thus end up on the front pages of the same newspapers that his own audience hate but which everyone reads.

Similarly, the question of Grillo's populism is more complex than usually presented. Meaning: his is truly a neo-populism, in the strict sense. Perhaps there is no other movement or political figure to which Cas Mudde's definition more fully applies. The (Manichean) counterposition between the 'pure people' and the corrupt 'political class'; the straightforward dismissal of all official political society in the name of a direct appeal to the sovereign people (well expressed in the 'Surrender!' so loudly demanded on the eve of the vote, in near-messianic tones); the substitution of the old horizontal Left/Right distinction with the vertical top/bottom one, and the movement's insistence on its much-proclaimed transversal character; the assumption of the role of advocates for all those expropriated of power, as against the bureaucratic, financial and party oligarchies – all of this marks out a very clear profile. But it would be hard to attach it to other contemporary forms of populism that go under this same label (as the media and its political rivals generally do). Nor could it easily be assimilated by these others, notwithstanding some of the Five Star leadership's political choices (for instance, its joining EFDD, the group in the European Parliament led by Nigel Farage).

Testament to these differences are the many battles fought in the Movement's gestation period – for the environment, for peace, for participation and against authoritarianism. But so, too, are the contents of the programme on which it stood in the general election, which was clearly distinct and, in many regards, opposed to that of the various parties and movements of the European (and Western) populist Right. Roberto Biorcio has emphasised this with great clarity in a work based on telling empirical data. For Biorcio, the identity of the greater part of the contemporary neo-populism is strongly oriented toward the demand for a restoration of 'sovereignty' – entrusted 'to a "strong leader" able to make the will of the common people felt in the institutions'. Indeed, 'the idea of "the people" which is postulated is characterised in a strongly ethnic and nationalist sense', in which immigrants and Roma people are taken for enemies (and in Italy this kind of neo-populism would be typified by the Lega and the post-fascist Fratelli d'Italia). Yet 'the programme constructed by the M5S is completely different, and almost the opposite to this'. Its objectives 'are above all oriented to encouraging participative citizen democracy, defending a universalist welfare state, and protecting and championing common and/or public goods (citizens' income and standing for investment in school and public healthcare)'.[24]

This is backed up by a post-election survey, cited by Biorcio, from which it emerges that it is among Five Star voters that we can record the highest level of agreement with the statement that one of the government's priority goals should be the reduction of 'differences of income among citizens' (54 per cent of M5S voters agreed, against 47 per cent of PD voters, 40 per cent of PdL voters and 13 per cent of Lega voters)[25] and 'guaranteeing stable social protections'.[26] Conversely, M5S voters expressed limited demand for a 'strong leader' (5 per cent below the average for all

---

24   Biorcio, *Il populismo nella politica italiana*, p. 105.

25   Itanes post-election study, ibid., p. 106.

26   54.4 per cent of Five Star voters replied positively to this question, against 50.6 per cent of voters for the PD, 50 per cent for the Lega and 45 per cent for the PdL.

voters) and, at the same time, the lowest degree of 'confidence' in the European Union to be found among any party's supporters.[27] And indeed 'confidence' (as both a mood and an orientation for action) is central to the clearest difference – we could even say, the most important cleavage – that distinguishes the Five Star electorate from other sociopolitical 'worlds', and in particular the PD's. This applies to both 'confidence in institutions' – for which Five Star voters express the lowest scores, close to zero, while PD voters are at the top of the scale; and 'confidence in the future' (in socio-economic terms) – the Five Star vote is polarised among the most pessimistic (and those who were most sacrificed by the crisis) while the PD electorate is concentrated among the optimistic (and evidently, the most well-at-heel or, in any case, hit least hard). This, fundamentally, is the key to the *grillino* success, which is not easily dented, notwithstanding the errors, the shortfalls, the gaffes and the inexperience displayed by the 'political personnel' of this 'non-party'. And notwithstanding an *in extremis* attempt, on an unexpected front, to make a breakthrough on M5S's own terrain.

Matteo Renzi's 'populism from above'

The idea itself was not all that bad: to try to intercept the shifts in a liquid electorate as it leaked out of the crisis-ridden party containers and an exhausted political-institutional system, using a second-hand 'populist style' to capture these flows within a form of governance compatible with the system's own balances

---

27 Only 34 per cent of Five Star voters have 'confidence in the European Union', against 59 per cent of voters for the PD, 45 per cent for the PdL and 45 per cent for the Lega.

and above all the EU's 'social order'. Essentially, to try to build a veil of mass support beneath the 'automatic pilot' operation evoked by Mario Draghi immediately after the shock of the February 2013 election – an instrument that could still function, Draghi told us, whatever the post-electoral balance in parliament.

To try to build a popular and electoral base through a typically populist use of rhetoric and (apparently) transgressive behaviours that serve to legitimise ('down below') policies which substantively conform to political inclinations willed and dictated 'from above' and, moreover, serve the possibility of using institutional apparatuses that would otherwise have been difficult to handle.

This was, on closer inspection, the meaning of the Renzian experiment – of his 'governmental populism'. This was the reason why the Letta government was killed off so abruptly, once again through an action that took place outside of parliament. Letta's cabinet was considered in all likelihood to be too lacking in popular support to be able to bear the weight of the interventions in the social and institutional orders which it had been called on to make. But, in many regards, Matteo Renzi is a 'populist'. One of a new type, of course. A post-twentieth-century, post-ideological, post-democratic populist. He also differs from the other contemporary 'neo-populists': certainly, he is no 'identitarian populist' like the emerging central European ethnonationalisms, but nor is he a 'social-protest'-oriented populist, to again use Taguieff's classification.[28]

---

28   Pierre-André Taguieff distinguishes between 'an "identitarian" or "national-identitarian" pole – whether this retravels the paths of xenophobic paleonationalism or takes form as a variant of the emerging ethnonationalism, in reaction to some figure of financial globalisation or cultural

This is, rather, a 'hybrid' populism,[29] with little struggle and a little government. It remixes the ingredients of Italy's other previous populisms. In the decision to speak 'directly to citizens' using the TV or other media, there is a pinch of Berlusconian 'telepopulism', with an impressive proliferation of promises to resolve all the problems that the parties and politicians have never managed to confront.[30] And there is another pinch of *grillino* 'anti-caste' populism, deployed with the rhetoric of 'scrapping the establishment' – an extremely aggressive concept (almost like Five Star's 'Vaffanculo Day'). This latter is levelled against his own party rivals, the 'old guard' guilty precisely of being old, gout-afflicted and lethargic, but also against the old 'left-wing' ideas – the old, never completely digested identity of the 'new Party'. This polemic is useful for speaking to an outside electorate, of the centre or even the Right. It is promising for whoever has a view to building a true 'Party of the Nation' (the dream of any good populist). And it also helped turn the second primaries to Renzi's advantage, in a vote which would crown him leader of an ever more personalised party. As well as being very much in a Florentine *stil novo* (new style), placed in service of a 'pop politics' taken to the limit of aesthetic elaboration.

This explains Renzi's presence on light entertainment programmes (dressed as 'Fonzie' on Maria de Filippi's show or chatting with Barbara d'Urso like Berlusconi used to). Shirt sleeves adopted as a uniform. The smartphone always in his hand,

---

and communicative mondialisation' and, on the other hand, 'a "protest" or "social-protest" pole'. The former is centred on *ethnos*, and the latter on *demos* (*L'illusion populiste*, p. 177).

29 Taguieff applies this label to 1980s British Thatcherism.

30 Biorcio, *Il populismo nella politica italiana*, p. 123.

chatting like a teenager. The quick march. The meetings of the party leadership at 7am. The unseemly but knowing phrases of an *enfant terrible* ('the new Ulivo [centre-left coalition] brings only a yawn; it's time to take a wrecking-ball to our leaders').

And then that first speech as prime minister (his 'inauguration' address) before the Senate which he was getting ready to demolish: the hand in his pocket, speaking off the cuff, his eyes fixed not on the parliamentary benches but on the TV cameras and the invisible audience that lay beyond, not to mention the low level of the speech's very content. The whole staging of the speech revealed an (in fact, never concealed) intention to bypass the 'circle' of institutional representatives and directly address the generic 'stalls' of what he considered 'his' people. In a sense he sought to humiliate the former (downgraded to a 'caste' to be liquidated sooner or later, to a mere dead weight) in order to satisfy the latter, to whom he made a nod and a wink. In a sense, to produce the sensation of a *novum*. And indeed, we had never previously seen a chief of the Executive turn directly to the people as against a branch of the legislature that he was himself preparing to make redundant. It was as if Grillo had moved into the prime minister's residence and was using it to mobilise his network to 'send them all home'.

In part, Renzi's gambit did succeed. The results of the May 2014 European elections seemed to endorse his approach: the 40.8 per cent won by the PD, a few months after Renzi became the head of government, included an audience wider than the party's traditional reservoir of support, with the arrival of part of the centre (many from Mario Monti's Scelta civica, but not only them) and even the Right (if also losing some to the Left), a considerable influx of practising Catholics (much better-represented than they had been in the PD's Bersani era), and even some from the Five Star Movement and former abstainers. As was written at the time, 'Renzi's refined populism has drawn the embrace of the crowd. The prime minister's open-minded style seems to please.'[31] But even the most sophisticated operations in political marketing and electoral restyling met their limit in a series of material factors, of biographical, social, relational and anthropological (in the broad sense) dimensions. It is problematic to 'invent oneself' as a populist through exercises in style alone. Or through exercises in rhetoric that have no raw material to deal with, such as might come from one's origins or one's 'popular' nature. Renzi's *cursus honorum* was in fact typical of a career politician; as a very young man he was a provincial secretary of the Partito Popolare, and he hardly passed via any other trade. His social origin was among local notables, with constant intersections with local politics and small financial interests. His associates were all in the higher ranks of the social pyramid: CEOs like Sergio Marchionne, international brokers like Serra, entrepreneurs *à la page* like Oscar Farinetti, directors of global investment banks like Jamie Dimon at J.P. Morgan . . . the appointments at Florence's Leopolda resembled smaller-scale versions of the World Economic Forum at Davos or the Italian business leaders' summit at Cernobbio. And, as for his practical policies, they were more reminiscent of the implementation of the list of requests (or rather, orders) contained in Trichet and

31   Federico Geremicca, 'Il populismo raffinato di Renzi raccoglie l'abbraccio della folla', *La Stampa*, 3 June 2014. 'The applause, the photos and the "give me fives" of Renzian stamp have now been definitively legitimised even in the oh-so-serious halls of power in Rome', the text continued. 'How long is it since a political leader was last surrounded by such popular sympathy. Moreover: how long since one could last walk among the population without risking booing, insults or, tragically, even coins being thrown?'

Draghi's 2011 letter, or a Troika memorandum, than a programme liable to enjoy popular support. And they always had the enthusiastic support of the employers' association Confindustria and the chancelleries of Europe – Merkel first among them – the financial institutions and the main international agencies. That is, of all the establishment forces on the ground both within and outside Italy. Only the 80 euro a month tax break debated in the immediate lead-up to the European elections – 'in perfect populist style', as has been observed, seemed to reduce the distance between the words used and the policies put into effect.

'Dies irae'

The *experimentum crucis* would come in December 2016, around his thousandth day in government, with the referendum on the 'mother of all reforms': the vote on Renzi's planned changes to the Italian Constitution. A test that Renzi – and how could it have been otherwise – confronted in perfect populist style. This was true from the very formulation of the referendum questions, from their very grammar, structured around the triple matrix of populist themes: cutting the cost of politics ('curtailing the costs of institutions' functioning'), an eternal battlehorse of all populisms of whatever colour; 'cutting the number of parliamentarians', the oft-asserted call to cut the famous 'politicians' armchairs'; the abolition of pointless quangos, with the presently invisible CNEL held up for the media's derision; the simplification of administrative procedures, reduced to the simplistic solution of altering Titolo V and cutting local autonomy. A wishlist, we could say, with more of a marketing logic than one focused on the constitutionally guaranteed establishment of direct democracy.

Also revealling was the long gestation period for the constitutional reform. There were repeated attacks on the dissenting or even just doubtful voices of authoritative constitutionalists and jurists who were dismissed as 'eggheads', 'old owls' and 'bitter types'. This, in tune with an 'anti-culturalist' style, denigrating intellectuals, and which is rooted in the populist attitude and the tradition of *qualunquismo*. This was added, naturally, to the long referendum campaign and the slogans widely propagated by the prime minister himself, personally entering the fray like no chief of the Italian government ever had done before. The use of hyperbole, of extreme simplification, of *damnatio personae* and the attempt to present any rival positions as ridiculous, dismissed as do-nothing blockages to action, the peremptory ultimatums, the anti-caste slogans. Effectively, the whole repertoire of populist rhetoric was put on display: 'If No wins, it will be a victory for those who put up vetoes (for many, to avoid giving up their privileges)' (Matteo Renzi, Ancona, 30 November); 'Those who vote No are taking the caste as it is!' (Matteo Renzi, 30 November); 'It's not about Yes or No, but Yes or never. This is citizens' opportunity to change things' (Matteo Renzi, 30 November #bastaunsi); 'On Sunday [referendum day], it's up to you, friends, if you want to vote No and keep the armchairs like before, because it's not about voting for me but for our children' (Matteo Renzi, 30 November at #Matrix) . . . Right up to the grand finale in his own city of Florence on 2 December: 'The future begins with a Yes. There is a silent majority that wants to be taken in hand in order to change the future'; 'If Yes wins, Italy will become a European leader and not a cash machine for those who take in money and lose their humanity'.

His thrashing at the ballot box – a clear 60–40 margin (59.1 per cent to 40.9 per cent, to be precise) – tells us that this operation did not succeed – that the 'populism from above' he had experimented with for almost three years crashed up against a popular will surging from below, in stubborn opposition. It was almost as if in that vote, through a sort of political nemesis, the champions of the reform and the main sponsors of the referendum had been forced back within the ranks of the muchdeprecated elite (one left in the minority), and the People had taken back its own autonomy from the Government. Again in this case – as in the Brexit referendum and the various other electoral contests which we have considered already – the 'electoral geography' was itself telling. And it speaks more the language of the diffuse suffering that spread under the surface of Renzi's exalted narrative, almost without making any upsurge or outcry of its own, than that of articulated party-political belonging (indeed, media would define it 'more a social than a political vote').[32] In fact, the map of the No vote faithfully retraces the map of malaise; or better, of the different social, generational and territorial forms of malaise. The No vote grew exponentially where disposable income was lowest, where unemployment – and in particular youth unemployment – was greatest, as we move from the centre to the periphery of the big cities, and, naturally, the further South.

According to the Quorum study for Italy's second all-news channel Sky TG24, some 81 per cent of young people voted No, whereas Piepoli give a figure of 68 per cent (only among elderly Italians did Yes win, albeit by a narrow margin: the pollsters

---

32   See Renato Benedetto, 'I giovani bocciano la riforma: il 68 per cent degli under 35 ha votato no. I dati dell'Istituto Piepoli per la Rai. Più alta la percentuale di Quorum per Sky Tg24. Un voto più "sociale" che "politico" ', *Corriere della Sera*, 6 December 2016.

give, respectively, 51 per cent to 49 per cent or 53 per cent to 47 per cent among over-fifty-fives).[33] As for socio-professional categories, the greatest percentage for No was recorded among the unemployed and workless (78 per cent, according to Ipsos), followed by blue-collar and related groups (70 per cent), public employees and the self-employed (68 per cent and 67 per cent); the best results for Yes (that is, above the general average) were among pensioners, housewives, and the category made up of businessmen, professionals and managers.[34] A study by the Istituto Cattaneo that analysed the specific results in the city of Bologna, one of the few places, indeed, where Yes did win, shows that voters grouped in the lowest income bracket, under €18,000 a year (51.3 per cent) mostly opted for No, while those with incomes over €25,000 a year gave a clear Yes vote (60 per cent).[35]

At the same time, one cannot but be struck by the electoral cartography elaborated by Ipsos,[36] with a map of Italy in which the few dark-green spots (the only provinces where Yes secured

---

33 In both the Quorum survey for Sky Tg24 and the one by Piepoli: 'Referendum, l'analisi del voto: i flussi dei partiti e le tendenze per fasce di età. L'esame dei flussi elettorali. Tornata alle urne una quota degli astenuti alle Europee', *Corriere della Sera*, 6 December 2016. All the others were located in between the two: for Ipsos, 18–34 and 35–49-year-olds gave above average No votes, at 64 per cent and 67 per cent respectively, while the older age groups gave a below average No vote, 57 per cent.

34 47 per cent, 43 per cent and 41 per cent, respectively.

35 Istituto Carlo Cattaneo, *Referendum 4 dicembre 2016 – Referendum 'sociale' o costituzionale? Torna il problema delle 'periferie' per il Pd*, analysis under the direction of Carlo Valbruzzi, 5 December 2016.

36 Ipsos Public Affairs, *Referendum costituzionale 2016 – Analisi post-voto*, 5 December 2016, ipsos.it.

a clear victory) are concentrated in a strip through central Italy (especially Florence, Siena and Arezzo, as well as Modena and Ravenna) as well as Bolzano, while the rest of the North and Centre is red or pink (indicating the varying hues of No's success, in the range between 51 per cent and 60 per cent), while the South and the Islands are a bright brick red, indicating percentages sometimes even far higher than the national average, up to the ceiling of 73–4 per cent reached in Sicily and Sardinia. The regions, that is, where the unemployment rate is highest, GDP is lowest and both absolute and relative poverty levels are most explosive. For example, No was as high as 68.3 per cent in Naples; 69.4 per cent in Taranto; 72.3 per cent in Palermo. In Rome, it only got (so to speak) 59.4 per cent, but in Municipio VI, on the far eastern periphery of the capital (the so-called 'torri' of Torspaccata, Torre Maura, Torre Angela and Tor Vergata) where there is a large population today in dire straits, No came as high as 71 per cent; in Municipio X on the southern periphery of the capital it scored 65 per cent, and 62 per cent in neighbouring Municipio XI. Only in Parioli, the very smartest neighbourhood of Rome, did Yes eke out a victory with 50.5 per cent. As Enzo Fortunato of the Brothers of Assisi – director of Sanfrancesco. org magazine – commented, 'This was the No of poor families who struggle to make it to the end of the month and who are tired of politics. The Country [*Paese*] was vetoed by the small towns [*paesi*]'.

Conversely, the map of 'party loyalties' reveals a much blurrier and more fluid picture. As has been written, the classic political containers 'cracked open' in the referendum vote, allowing a considerable part of their contents to escape: for instance, according to the Quorum study around a quarter of the voters who had backed the PD in 2014 opted for No; making up for this, a similar percentage of Forza Italia voters turned in favour of Yes, contravening Silvio Berlusconi's own indications. More than half of NCD (a small centre-right party which was allied to the PD in government in 2013–18) voters broke with the party line and voted against the reform, while in the opposite direction a sizeable part of the voter base of Scelta Civica voted Yes despite its leader (and 2011–13 prime minister) Mario Monti's declaration for No.

If for no other reason than the difficulty of the established political containers in holding together, and the strong social connotation of the geography of the vote, one could draw parallels between the Italian referendum and its clamorous result with what we may consider to be its British twin. Such a characterisation of the resounding defeat of the government's proposal would ultimately mean including the Italian case in the map of the now-widespread political and institutional instability that is an expression of the 'populist syndrome'. A similar reading has been proposed by many commentators across almost all parts of the political spectrum, and one cannot hide the fact that there do exist telling analogies, at least in formal terms, in the distribution of the dissent. So, too, in the electorate's impermeability to the pressures and the incitement that came from a media universe largely aligned with the establishment and with solutions promising 'order'. Equally, in the widespread rejection of this same establishment, implicit in the message given by the electorate with their vote 'against the current'. Indeed, the electoral maps and the coloration of this referendum vote almost perfectly overlap with that of the spring 2018 general election. The shifts of voters away from the PD and Forza Italia in December 2016 would swell the growth of both the Five Star Movement and the Lega just over a year later, ensuring these forces' victory over two populisms more scarred (and decrepit) by previous periods in government (in both Renzi's case and Berlusconi's). The winners were the 'oppositional' populisms of those who had been in some way 'against' what went before: the rebellious and Southern-focused populism of the *grillini* (M5S) and the Lega's 'regional' populism now converting into a national (or rather, nationalist) force and thus transforming into a sort of plebeian heir to Berlusconi's exhausted populism, regenerating it through a new rebellious charge.

What arose in March's vote is a sociopolitical ferment made up of more than 50 per cent of those who turned out to vote. Such is the 'yellow-green' government's base of support, and surveys in autumn 2018 show it rising yet further to around 60 per cent. As we have seen, internally, this base is socially and geographically heterogeneous, but it is united by a common demand for some kind of radical change (and indeed the government that emerged from the 'political contract' signed by the two parties in June defines itself 'the government of change'). It is characterised by a drastic rejection of all previous experiences. This is, to use an old saying, a populism 'of struggle and of government', weaving together 'securitarian' policies with (more timidly advanced) 'social' ones. It carries a distinct whiff of 'sovereigntyism' (reflecting the demands of the Lega's nationalist positions), along with a social-reformist aftertaste (expressing the M5S's own positions). In this sense, it is a 'bipolar' populism, both as that term is used in the political vocabulary (it involves two different and diverse political cultures that may potentially be in conflict) and as it is used in psychiatric pathology (the expression of a 'mood disorder' focused on the emotional sphere). A 'syncretic' and 'recuperative' populism, the product of an unprecedented synthesis of the previous populisms on this peninsula will ensure its endurance in government through its dynamic activity, as it capitalises on the absence of credible alternatives that has been left behind by the other, now-exhausted populisms. The most appropriate analogy might be that of the exploding supernova that leaves behind a yawning black hole.

Conclusion:

The Age of the Void

Perhaps there are good reasons why Italy has so long been a terrain of experimentation for a series of political experiences that can all, despite their differences, be related back to the neo-populist matrix. Italy has the track record, both in terms of the longevity of these experiences – for more than two decades – and in terms of the multiplicity of forms its populist expressions have taken. This might be surprising, if we look only at the institutional 'surface' of politics. But it is not such a shock when we dig a little deeper and consider even fleetingly a few structural realities.

One salient example of such realities is the fact that, for almost a quarter of a century, Italy's industrial base and economic strength have been travelling along a downward slope, experiencing what is so brutally termed the country's 'decline'. Among the OECD countries – the so-called 'developed' economies – no country has done worse in dealing with the epochal leap represented by the exhaustion of the 'Fordist' sequence and the transition to a new paradigm that is no longer centred on mass industrial production but on highly competitive manufacturing and the supply of services by an advanced tertiary sector. Already before the great crisis, Italy had lost a good part of its industrial apparatus, or at least, of its backbone.[1] Between 1990 and 2007, real GDP almost flatlined, while real GDP per capita decreased constantly. Mean family incomes fell almost 5 per cent relative to the European average in just a few years. Wages remained at a standstill. And the poverty rate was already by 2007–8 among the worst in the Eurozone. The wave of crisis in 2008–9 did the rest, as a downpour fell on an already soaked land and the reservoir of malaise swelled enormously.

We see fine evidence of this in a troubling report by the well-known agency McKinsey & Co., one of the great ideological motors of globalisation, which can normally be counted on to be optimistic about the fate of the 'new world' but which in this case showed uncharateristic signs of concern. This report, entitled *Poorer than their parents?*, investigated the 'flat and falling incomes in advanced economies'.[2] It portrayed a landscape that was not only realistic but also troubling; the mass media commented on its findings in pieces with such telling titles as 'The Death of the Middle Class Is Worse Than You Think'.[3] It shows how the exponential growth in inequalities across the whole globalised West between 2005 and 2014 opened up an outright social chasm, and that in twenty-five advanced economies between 65 and 70 per cent of citizens had seen their incomes flatline or fall: which is to say, a mass of between 540 and 580 million people who feel themselves being pushed to the margins or losing their class position. Of these, just 10 million – a tiny 2 per cent – had

---

1 Luciano Gallino highlighted this already in 2003, writing that Italy had 'almost totally lost its industrial capacity' and that this would 'fall to zero if the car industry also went' (*La scomparsa dell'Italia industriale*, Einaudi, Turin 2003).

2 McKinsey Global Institute, *Poorer Than Their Parents? Flat or Falling Incomes in Advanced Economies*, McKinsey & Co, July 2016.

3 Chris Matthews, 'The Death of the Middle Class Is Worse Than You Think', *Fortune*, 14 July 2016.

reported in 2005 that they had remained at a standstill or become poorer over the previous decade, between 1993 and 2004. This is telling of the extensive effects of the social earthquake that has shaken the entire developed West during the crisis period. And it tells us of the structural earthquake suffered by the countries involved, necessarily combined with a parallel change in the political landscape, of greater or lesser violence depending on how close that country is to the epicentre of the quake.

The report goes on to demonstrate that the great freeze has not hit everyone in a homogeneous way – that some countries have been hit more violently, and that Italy is by far the worst case, with the largest proportion of the population having become impoverished, some 97 per cent of families, followed by the United States with 81 per cent and the United Kingdom with 70. France is doing a little better, with 63 per cent *déclassés*, while Sweden is outside the danger zone, with only 20 per cent pushed toward the margins. This map of malaise, which takes account of the reduction in both 'disposible income' and 'market income', can almost entirely be traced onto the map of the insurgent political phenomena classified as 'populism'. And this malaise applies to both 'capital's side' (in particular financial investment and productive activities) and 'labour's side'. The former was hit by the conjunctural effects of the crisis and the latter was already heavily penalised relative to capital by structural transformations which had been taking place during the long gestation period that preceded the subprime explosion. Two researchers from the Bank for International Settlements (BIS) had shown this already in 2007, before the involutional cycle described by McKinsey even began, in a study devoted to the gradual shifts in the ratio of profits to wages in the composition of the main industrialised countries' GDP between the early 1990s and the mid-2000s.[4]

From this we see that, in around two decades, between 8 and 10 per cent of GDP shifted from total wages to total profits: an enormous figure, which amounts to around €120 billion a year that is no longer present in workers' pay packets (as it would have been if the wages/profits ratio had remained as it was) and which has instead become available to companies (which have often deployed them in financial circuit rather than in productive investment). Other, subsequent studies have corrected the numbers (with even worse figures for waged labour) as the weight of financialisation and the 'production of money through money' has increased. In the Italian case, this has brought labour's 'deficit' and its social marginalisation to the brink of €200 million a year. This indicates the historic, and essentially silent, defeat it has suffered, without deliberation or self-reflection by the same social and political forces who in the twentieth century took responsibility for leading and representing labour. Yet it is a defeat that is destined to weigh on mass behaviours and on 'political realignments', and offers us a further tile in the complex sociopolitical mosaic, as we attempt to interpret and reclassify the forms of social protest, including the one often dismissed (or exorcised) as 'populist'.

A few years ago, Luciano Gallino published a lively interview-book entitled 'The Class Struggle after the Class Struggle',[5] a phrase to refer to the 'war' declared from above – by capital – against that which stood below, labour (hence the reference to an 'after' and a change of direction). Capital sought to take back – with interest, we could say – what had been won by labour, in terms

---

4   Luci Ellis and Kathryn Smith, 'The global upward trend in the profit share', Working Paper no. 231, Bank for International Settlements, July 2007.

5   Luciano Gallino, *La lotta di classe dopo la lotta di classe*, interview edited by Paola Borgna, Laterza, Roma-Bari 2012.

of income and rights, during the previous cycle of industry and of conflict, in the 'social twentieth century'. The sociologist, attentive to the numbers and their significance, maintained that this struggle had been won by those who stood up above, also thanks to a genetic mutation in their own order, which turned in favour of the abstract dimension of capital, which is to say to its monetary dimension. And such a conclusion can hardly be challenged, having been confirmed year after year in news reports and the latest statistics. Almost all of us, convinced by this diagnosis from the outset, concentrated most of our attention on what followed from this mutation of those forces 'up above': on the formation of new oligarchies, on the destructiveness of finance capital and its changeable global oligarchies, on the *modus operandi* of the postmodern robber barons, on the socially destructive use of monetary policies and austerity. There was rather less reflection on what was happening 'down below'. That is to say, on the repercussions of this 'historic defeat' in the belly of the metropoles and in the former industrial districts where the strength of the twentieth-century workers' movement had been concentrated. As if these pieces of social composition had, as in the thought of Benedetto Croce,[6] departed from the course of History, instead to return to a state of Nature. We failed to ask ourselves what 'subjectivity' was taking form in that 'global below'.

Now we do see it. This historical protagonist had once fed the symbolism and the imaginary as well as the electoral support and the organisational apparatus of all the combined forces of the Left in the 'labour century'. Today, it is a major (perhaps not majority, but certainly steadfast) part of the hardcore of the vast galaxy in

---

6   The Italian philosopher renowned for his 'idealist historicism' which counterposed History to Nature and considered progress as Man's emancipation from Nature, so as himself to become the protagonist of History.

which today's neo-populist insurgency expresses itself. Added to this insurgency, in recent years, is the heterogeneous mass of what had traditionally been Western societies' principal 'ballast', a force for balance, stability and 'moderation', that is, the middle class, the representative democracies' own 'white guard'. It is now impoverished, wounded and *déclassé* not so much by wage cuts and the marginalisation of labour (though in part also by this) but above all by the reversing fortunes of financial annuities during the crisis. During its ascendant phase, finance capitalism offered these annuities as compensation for the standstill in income from labour: hence the boundless growth of Wall Street, the use of lending and house sales as a monetary lever for families themselves, the hedge fund prices of which they knew nothing. And, from 2008, they began to devour their own owners (the small, the inexpert, cut out of insider trading, who had trusted in their broker and their bank).

Altogether, they form a multitude of the dissatisfied and enranged – above all, the 'betrayed', or those who consider themselves as such – transversally distributed across Western societies, extraneous to the traditional political cultures since none of them still represent the new conditions of the masses. These latter are themselves out of place, as they find themselves in the unpredcedented condition of the politically homeless. Humiliated by the distance that they see growing between themselves and the few who stand at the top of the pyramid (despite their small numbers, the only ones visible in the media space that has replaced all previous public spaces). Lacking in a language suitable for communicating their own stories, or even to structure an account of themselves, they are thus consigned to resentment and rancour. They are the 'people of victims' discussed in philosophical terms by Slavoj Žižek; they feed the diffuse feeling of rage, unease and suspicion that has descended on ever more liquid and agitated societies. This, after the ultimate default of responsibility of the extraordinary 'banks of rage' (as another philosopher, Peter Sloterdijk, called them) that were the old parties of the Left and, at the same time, the churches: the 'noble' instruments that allowed the bottling up of the desire for vendetta and revenge for the (social) injustices suffered, instead promising that they would, in time, be satisfied.

Today, in a world that has become universally, dramatically unequal, in which as few as eight super-rich individuals possess the equivalent of the resources of half of humanity, and in which – as the latest Oxfam report tells us[7] – we are now expecting the advent of the first trillionaire (someone whose assets exceed a thousand billion dollars),[8] we find no political protagonist, no candidate to represent these 'losers of the new economy' who is able to credibly put themselves forward as the instrument of a battle for equality. In most countries, the postbox of egalitarian policies lies empty. What comes to pass is that the army of losers entrust themselves to a winner, so long as he is able to give voice to their rage and offer an alternative. To a billionaire like Trump, because he is coarse and aesthetically different from the elite. To a successful demagogue like Boris Johnson, who belongs to the highest ranks of London

---

7   Oxfam, *An Economy for the 99 per cent. It's time to build a human economy that benefits everyone, not just the privileged few*, Oxfam Briefing Papers, January 2017. The eight billionaires are Bill Gates (the American principal founder of Microsoft), Amancio Ortega (the Spanish owner of Zara), Warren Buffett (the American shareholder and CEO of Berkshire Hathaway), Carlos Slim Helu (the Mexican owner of the Grupo Carso), Jeff Bezos (American, president of Amazon), Mark Zuckerberg (American, co-founder of Facebook), Larry Ellison (American, co-founder and CEO of Oracle), and Michael Bloomberg (American, founder and owner of Bloomberg Lp).

8   As the Oxfam report observes, it would take a million dollars' spending a day for 2,738 years to eat up this fortune – and that is not counting the composite interest on capital, and any other investment.

society but is capable of deploying plebeian tones on TV. Or indeed to Theresa May herself, if it seems that she gives voice to a post-imperial revanchism shot-through with social grievance.

Almost everywhere, the neo-populist agitation *from below* is openly exploited by those who in fact stand *up above*, without any seeming contradiction. And perhaps this explains the reason why Europe's governing elites, and with them the greater part of the 'system's information system', in fact dedicate themselves much more energetically and effectively to fighting and destabilising the only experiences that have proven a convincing and credible factor for combating this type of contagion. This, even as they fake fear and indignation over these upheavals and stigmatise them with anathemas which – precisely because of where the preaching is coming from – merely strengthen their following. We need only think of the indecent treatment, fierce in both form and content, that Europe's powers-that-be imposed on Greece – indeed, a treatment very different from that reserved for figures like the 'national-populist' Orbán in his barbed-wire Hungary, or the freedom-killing President Erdogan in Turkey. Or the attempts to isolate Podemos in Spain, as the declining social-democratic parties of Europe shift toward a conservative centre that is subaltern to the restrictive policies demanded by Berlin and Brussels.

Yet perhaps we needed some clear warning signs to at least partly ignite the timebombs in the looming post-democratic future. That is, to make us talk again about redistributive policies, accessible social services, a health system that is not reduced to shreds, a less punitive wage dynamic, policies less buried in the dogma of austerity. What was once called 'reformism' and yet now seems so 'revolutionary'.

But as we know, 'Whom the gods would destroy they first make mad'.

Index

Index

Index

Index